MAS $40 \underline{\underline{00}}$

1st U

D0894738

SCHOLAR MOUNTAINEERS
PIONEERS OF PARNASSUS

By the same author:

MOUNTAINS AND MEN

SCHOLAR MOUNTAINEERS

PIONEERS OF PARNASSUS

WILFRID NOYCE

With wood-engravings by R. Taylor

London

DENNIS DOBSON LTD

First published in Great Britain in MCML by
DENNIS DOBSON LTD, 12 Park Place, St James's, London
SW1. All rights reserved. Printed in Great Britain by
WESTERN PRINTING SERVICES LTD, Bristol.

193/R

CONTENTS

	INTRODUCTORY	9
I	HEIGHTS AND DEPTHS IN DANTE	23
II	PETRARCA ALPINISTA	35
III	THE SENTIMENTALITY OF ROUSSEAU	47
IV	DE SAUSSURE, PIONEER OF SCIENCE	57
V	GOETHE, THE ROMANTIC MAN	69
VI	THE WORDSWORTHS	81
VII	JOHN KEATS	93
VIII	JOHN RUSKIN AND THE AESTHETIC APPROACH	103
IX	LESLIE STEPHEN	115
X	NIETZSCHE AND MODERN MOUNTAINEERING	127
XI	THE RELIGIOUS VIEW AND POPE PIUS XI	139
XII	ROBERT FALCON SCOTT: THE ANTARCTIC TRAGEDY	149
	A SHORT BIBLIOGRAPHY	163

LIST OF ILLUSTRATIONS

'The Foot of Purgatory' from the drawing by Sandro
　　Botticelli　　24

'The Valley of Vaucluse and the Slopes of Mont
　　Ventoux' from an old print　　40

'The House and Ridge at Les Charmettes' from
　　Visite aux Charmettes, Libraires Dardel　　48

'The Ascent to the Col du Géant' from a contem-
　　porary print　　64

'Faustus and Mephistopheles before the Brocken'
　　from *Faustus from the German of Goethe*, 1821　　72

'Grasmere seen from Loughrigg': Photo by Wilfrid
　　Noyce　　88

'John Keats' from *The Keats Letters*　　96

'The Cervin from the North-West side' from the
　　drawing by John Ruskin　　112

'The Schreckhorn and Finsteraarhorn': Photo by
　　Wilfrid Noyce　　120

'The Eiger North Wall'. 'Above it there stands
　　written "Impossibility"': Photo by Wilfrid
　　Noyce　　128

'Monte Rosa': Photo by Wilfrid Noyce　　144

'Mount Erebus as Wind Vane' from the drawing by
　　Dr E. A. Wilson (Courtesy the Scott Polar
　　Research Institute)　　152

ACKNOWLEDGEMENTS

Anything that I write owes its conception and form to the influence of other people. In this case I am grateful especially, over the whole series of essays, to Mrs H. W. Leakey and Professor A. C. Pigou; and to G. Winthrop Young for judgement and most valuable criticisms without which grave errors would have been allowed to stand. These have been attacked at any rate, if not obliterated.

In the individual sections I owe much to U. Limentani, N. Annan, R. J. Le Grand and T. H. Savory; and to Professor E. Vincent for suggestions as to illustration.

For the drawing of Mount Erebus I have to thank the Scott Polar Research Institute, Cambridge, and for old prints the Cambridge University Library.

WILFRID NOYCE

August 1949

Introductory

We are the Pilgrims, master; we shall go
Always a little further; it may be
Beyond that last blue mountain barred with snow
Across that angry or that glimmering sea.
JAMES ELROY FLECKER

THIS collection of mountain essays is not representative of mountaineering history. Nor does it add anything to the world's knowledge of the strange assembly of persons selected. For I have chosen from the records only what throws light on a single facet of their personality. I have considered them simply in relation to mountains. Most of them are figures about whom we think usually in very different connections, and they would be highly surprised at finding themselves set here together. They would all, except for Leslie Stephen, be still more astonished at being styled in any way fathers of our modern movement of mountaineering. Yet each has made his peculiar contribution to a certain feeling in us, a feeling which would not be quite the same had these men not lived. Without their example, our appreciation and our exertions among hills would be the weaker.

There is another link which binds them. Men of all ages have looked at mountains and have interpreted them in the light of their own social and religious needs. For each age

[9]

they have filled a gap to complete its picture, even when the
finishing touch needed was no more than a distant backcloth. Thus they have provided buttresses for theism, con-
solations to the atheist, weighty arguments to the cynic or
satisfying examples to the pantheist. Philosophers have
looked and have meditated, then they have pronounced
upon them. But behind their pronouncements the mountains stand still smiling and inscrutable. We will mean for
you what you wish, they seem to say. What we really are,
you can never know. This truth is illustrated by none better
than the writers here displayed. They come from different
countries and centuries; for at very few periods have the
mountains been held by the enlightened spirits as utterly
ugly or superfluous. In those few their dislike has at least
illuminated the character of the age itself. But this subject
would lead far afield and demand a book of worthier length
than this. For there are earlier days to be explored than
those of Dante, and farther lands than the boundaries of
Europe. We would need to inspect the Oriental, and particularly the Buddhist, attitude to mountains. The Himalaya
have remained a cornerstone of Buddhist worship. The
Buddhist seeks to escape Karma, the law of activity which
he must eschew even when that activity is not of itself bad.
This he does by contemplation, and contemplation of these
white and enormous masses will lead on to Meditation,
which is the last part of the eightfold path. Such is the
lesson of the sages Mila Repa and Marpa the translator.
Through contemplation, of a mountain for instance, the
idea of self can be lost and there is hope of entering Nirvana
or the divine nothingness.

'But the western mind', Leslie Stephen has written,
'refuses to lend itself long to such uncongenial efforts.
Thoughts of dinner . . .' Thoughts of life at any rate and
its active living begin to obtrude. We begin our European
record with the Greeks, and in Greece there is from the
first a typically western bustle upon the hilltops. The

Greeks did not need to be told that the noisy home of the
Gods should be upon Mount Olympus, the Judgement of
Paris on Mount Ida and their oracle at rocky Delphi; they
sensed a holiness in these places, because their instinct for
mountains came to them with the air they breathed. Thus
there are few direct references in their literature to the
association of man and mountain, but familiarity is chanted
from every chorus of Aeschylus's *Prometheus*. His epithets
pile as high as the rock towers themselves: 'A slippery,
lonely-hearted, eagle-haunted crag, that towers sheer
beyond the leap of goat, the gaze of man'. Nor was it for
nothing that the Bacchants were alleged to roam barefoot
over snowy Mount Taygetus. The Greeks reverenced
mountains as they reverenced the other natural sites which
were the obvious abode of gods. They interpreted them to
the pattern of their own pantheism.

The Romans went at the hills as hard-headedly as they
went at everything. They built their forts on precipices, if
precipices there chanced to be where they wanted forts, and
drove their roads up and down these interesting obstacles
to engineering skill. But they were heirs to the Greek tradition, and the mountain spirits, of all the Greek pantheon,
fitted best into their more rugged mythology. Their own
poor little Capitol they had early dignified with the title of
'Mons'. Later, they could see in the Alps and Apennines a
divinely placed bulwark or obstacle, according to the side
upon which you happened to be. And Rome too had her
poets. It was Virgil who hymned those Alps when he set
out to praise Italy; Virgil who, as a boy, was found wandering alone in a mountain cave; the first recorded pot-holer.
Horace gave, besides a love for the hilly Sabine farm, the
line

> *Vides ut alta stet nive candidum*
> *Soracte. . . .*

But Horace enjoyed his high mountains in a civilized way,
from a distance. And later the art of such enjoyment was

refined further by such as Pliny, who carefully arranged his sea villa to charm him with the vista of distant mountains.

Thus during the Empire the mountains retired to assume their rôle of backcloth. But the Romans were the last for many centuries to acknowledge these influences at all. When they departed the hilltops, forsaken by the Dryads, returned to misty obscurity until Dante came to set his earthly Paradise on their summit. But the strong currents of poetic feeling for hills which bubble through the *Divine Comedy*, or which drove Petrarch a few years later up the Mont Ventoux, spring as it were from isolated sources. In none of their contemporaries, and hardly in the Renaissance itself, was a lasting interest stirred. There were too many absorbing facets of the human life for scholars to spare more than a backward glance at distant heights. True, there were exceptional minds. Leonardo da Vinci touched a glacier and made scientific investigations. Antoine de Ville, Lord of Domp Julien, achieved at the King's command a perilous ascent of Mont Aiguille in the Dauphiné in 1492. Vadianus, the scholar, daringly ascended 'the very high mountain' Pilatus in 1518, and recorded the belief that Pilate appears every Good Friday dressed in his judge's robes upon its lakeside. Shakespeare's outlook embraced hills, as it embraced everything. Whatever Ruskin may say of his failure to appreciate all but the pine-tree tops, that poet was no stranger to the heights who could write:

> *to climb steep hills*
> *Requires slow pace at first,*

and:

> *even to the frozen ridges of the Alps*
> *Or any other ground inhabitable*
> *Wherever Englishman durst set his foot,*

and:

> *Full many a beauteous morning have I seen*
> *Flatter the mountain tops with sovereign eye.*

But the more general attitude of the age is exemplified in

the Jesuit Kirchner, of the seventeenth century, whose plan
it was to believe one-half of the legends told him about the
'horrid rocks'. For the hills had returned, after brief enlightenment, to be the abode of dragons and demons.
Kirchner was a traveller who accepted happily the story of
the man imprisoned for some months in a cave with two
dragons, and who finally escaped by holding on to their
tails when they flew away. He also saw that same lake on
Mount Pilatus where the Devil administers his annual
punishment to Pilate, and was 'gratified by discovering
certain suspicious footprints in the snow round its edge'.
Even, then, in these days of Sir Isaac Newton the mountains, in themselves considered ugly, were populated by
dragons and other romantic beings whose disappearance
before advancing science left them barren and unappetizing.
One explanation of the indifference, indeed dislike, of the
early eighteenth century is thus that no new interest had
yet appeared to take the place of the old awe. Science had
got so far as to reject dragons, after a brave attempt to
catalogue even these, but only gropingly with de Saussure
had it advanced far enough to substitute interest in moraines
and crevasses. Meanwhile it preferred green fields, with a
patchwork of human habitation.

It is not therefore surprising that at the turn of the century Bishop Burnet, who has some fine words to say about
these 'august and stately' objects, yet regards them as
nothing more than the ruins of a former world constructed
before the Deluge. They fitted very nicely with his theory
of the Creation. Nor is it wonderful that Dr Johnson, so
often typical of his age, confessed his unwillingness to be
dragged by a Boswell into this 'uniformity of Barrenness'.
'It will readily occur . . . that it is easy to sit at home and
conceive rocks, heaths and waterfalls, and that these journeys are useless labours, which neither impregnate the
imagination nor inform the understanding.' For there was
nothing left in the hills to drag men of sense like himself

towards them. He must, however, find some reason for having submitted to Boswell's persuasion; he can only conclude that man is here 'made unwittingly acquainted with his own weakness; and meditation shows him how little he can sustain, how little he can perform'. The emphasis therefore in his *Journey to the Hebrides* is upon man, on the manners of the Highland and other personalities whom they met. The mountains are useful as a yardstick by which to measure him. They are of no value in themselves. 'The hill behind the house we did not climb. The weather was rough, and the height and steepness discouraged us.' Description of the scenery would have been superfluous. Of Loch Lomond Boswell remarks: 'He was much pleased with the scene, which is so well known by the accounts of various travellers, that it is unnecessary for me to attempt any description of it'; and this though he has just had a very pretty shot at describing the rich and orderly Tallisker in the island of Skye. Perhaps had the weather been better they would have nodded more approvingly. Perhaps they would not have so severely strained each other's nerves, nor would the Doctor have shouted at his companion in fury for having got too far ahead. But at the very best the hills were permitted by the eighteenth-century scholars as a background to orderly human activity: the Savoy Alps smiled from a distance upon Gibbon, as he wrote the last words of his *Decline and Fall*. But at the idea of comparing them with the 'ideal prospect' of Charing Cross—Johnson would have snorted.

Chateaubriand, an early Romantic if ever there was one, went surprisingly far out of his way to denounce mountains as ugly lumps, and to detail the reasons for his verdict. But he was too late. It can be fairly said that the early eighteenth century was one of the few epochs which have genuinely regarded hills with disfavour; and even then, its writers wrung from them a setting for inns, like Dr Johnson, for books, like Gibbon, or for pleasing correspondence in the manner of Horace Walpole. Long before the century's end the tide was turning, and this owing to three main trends of feeling. Jean-Jacques Rousseau may have done very little active mountaineering himself, but he prepared the frame of mind which wanted to climb. He preferred to keep his own steps on lowlier hills. The height above Les Charmettes, on which he made his daily prayer, is the gentlest of gentle slopes. But he allows St Preux, the hero of his *La Nouvelle Héloïse*, to speak for him the sentiments which were to influence succeeding generations. St Preux can be more active: 'Under the conduct of a very honest guide I crawled up the towering hills through many a rough and unfrequented path.' At the top he meditates what can be the cause of his passion for heights. It is decided finally to be due in great part to the stimulating effect of mountain air. The real cause, for Rousseau, was of course that these rocks and ravines fitted with a doctrine of his own. He was using them to illustrate the truth that what is savage is noble, what is civilized must be corrupt. Thus the mountains returned to favour on a wave of doubtful theorizing. They represented 'Back to Nature', the enlightenment of the philosophic age or the revolt against the conventions. It mattered not at all that Rousseau's Nature was still a very mild, cardboard square human pattern, still set with green fields and always smiling at him.

The second of the waves which carried high hills to popularity was that of scientific inquiry. We left them reft of their dragons and demons but not yet the abode of any more substantial form of life. Horace Benedict de Saussure was one of the first to acknowledge in them, not maybe the relics of Burnet's antediluvian world, but at least a magnificent monument to ages before our own. His influence on the course of mountain climbing has been claimed with justification to have been greater than that of Rousseau. He was an aristocrat and a distinguished public figure in Geneva as well as 'creator of scientific Alpinism'. His public may have been smaller, but it was a more select one. The French critic Sainte-Beuve was right that 'Jean-Jacques had acquaintance only with the lowlands, the lakes, the cottages and orchards. . . . He never explored, or described in detail, even the middle zone. . . . The highest regions may be said to be the discovery and conquest of the famous scientist Saussure.' To him are owed the terms now used of everyday: 'sérac' and 'roche moutonnée', these are his bequest. To him is owed the fire of a love for truth which has illumined the best of mountain adventure since his day. For he linked passion and perspective as few others have done: the passion to climb Mont Blanc with the purpose of making scientific observations on its summit. But he bequeathed to poetry too something of the sacred scientific ardour: at any rate a love of accuracy in observation and phrasing which makes Wordsworth, and even the later Romantics, very much better guides than the earlier, glibly hyperbolical tourists.

After de Saussure, then, Wordsworth could describe with a naturalist's eye the bird and plant life of the Westmorland fells. Byron could studiously note how the

glacier's cold and restless mass
Moves onward day by day.

But besides all this and to return to our muttons, these writers still persisted in using their observations as a buttress to their own ideas. To Wordsworth the bare hills and their worthy inhabitants represent the ideal of life as ordained by a beneficent Creator. He could take that Nature which to Hardy was a wilderness of struggling, mutually slaughtering life, and after watching it carefully he could exclaim how evidently its author was both benign and omnipotent. The hills reveal manifestly the Divine Plan. Of the morning path up Snowdon he can exclaim:

There I beheld the emblem of a mind
That feeds upon infinity, that broods
Over the dark abyss.

Or he can extol the rural virtues with an optimism for

human nature that not the French Revolution itself had been able to damp. So it was with his contemporaries. There is among the poets of the early nineteenth century an increased love of description together with as great a desire to prop the mountains against their own worship or poetic theory. Goethe, the 'Romantic man', in whom every experience must find its place, was too diverse to allow their one aspect to dominate him. Yet he too must familiarize himself with them. He must, to begin with, overcome his aversion for heights, if only because he would otherwise be deprived of interesting geological studies and the examination of large buildings. He too therefore is ready to use hills, not only for scientific purposes but because they sympathize with his own poetic development from passionate youth to calm but interested old age.

Shelley among the English Romantics is more explicit even than Wordsworth. His desire is to have the mountains, Mont Blanc for instance, representative of the power which he personally wished to believe installed in Heaven:

> *Thou hast a voice, great mountain, to repeal*
> *Large codes of fraud and woe.*

Or he reads into them a lesson:

> *And this, the naked countenance of earth*
> *On which I gaze, even these primeval mountains,*
> *Teach the adverting mind.*

Coleridge's mountains, Leslie Stephen says, 'adduce excellent arguments in favour of theism'. Byron asks the delight of mountain storm, and sneers from his heights at the insignificance of mankind:

> *the glee*
> *Of the loud hills shakes with its mountain mirth.*

Or in France Lamartine demands permanence and the memory of his love:

> *O lac, rochers muets, grottes, forêt obscure!*
> *Vous que le temps épargne ou qu'il peut rajeuner,*
> *Gardez de cette nuit, gardez, belle nature,*
> *Au moins le souvenir!*

B

Or de Vigny finds on his Mount Sinai a source for his unquenchable pessimism. The mountains, assuredly, were already being exploited.

But there was still little enthusiasm among the littérateurs for the physical climbing of summits. Shelley looked at Mont Blanc and could remark contentedly, with no desire to seek further,

Power dwells apart in its tranquillity,
Remote, serene and inaccessible.

It is difficult to take too seriously his claim to have lived dangerously 'upon the brink of precipices' or to be acquainted with Alpine glaciers. When the ascents were made they were not always as competently handled as Wordsworth's. A poetic attempt on Fairfield, dumpiest of Lakeland lumps, by his contemporaries failed after a flash of exoticism: 'The leader's necessaries included a horse, a large tent, four bearers as well as four friends, 36 bottles of beer, two legs of lamb, two fowls, one tongue, half a pound of cigars, two packs of cards. . . . But they were defeated.' The tent was blown down, and not all the cheering that had ushered them out of Ambleside could persuade them to the top.

Shelley's attitude would have been approved heartily by John Ruskin, champion of the third movement, the aesthetic which was to re-establish mountain worship. The mountains were admitted by Ruskin as God's sanctuary because they were beautiful. But this was only so if they were treated as a temple, if they were approached with reverence and not used as 'greased poles'. The pictures of such painters as Turner had shown how beautiful they were. The religious impulse of all ages, of the Greeks with their Parnassus and the monks in their caves, had demonstrated their suitability as a shrine. And finally the scientific laws which governed everything, down to the streams upon Mont Blanc, marked the mutability and frailty of all temporal things.

But Ruskin remained something of a voice crying in the

wilderness claimed by his more energetic fellows. The gap between regard for hills as beautiful and desire for varied bodily exercise among them was already being bridged by the pioneers, climbing over the shoulders of scientists and aesthetes alike. The Alps had found, fortunately, a series of writers as convincing as they were cultured and charming: among them Edward Whymper, Leslie Stephen, Mummery, and later Geoffrey Winthrop Young. The sport may have owed its birth to an urge to 'conquer' the remaining strongholds of Nature, to a reaction from Victorian complacency or to the impulse to escape the Industrial Revolution. Whatever the origin, it was established. Queen Victoria herself ascended Lochnagar in 1848, sedately enough. She considered banning mountaineering as a 'dangerous eccentricity' after the 1865 tragedy, but she might have found difficulty in doing so. For the way was now open. Different voices summoned along different paths, but all among hills. British climbers still accepted the principle of caution and the sanctity of human life, even when they began to climb without guides. The voice of Nietzsche struck a new note, that of dangerous living sought expressly for its contribution to the attainment of Superman. This voice called towards the pessimism and habit of self-immolation of some of the Continental climbers between the wars, the 'pitoneers' who went cheerfully to their death on the north faces of the Eiger or Watzmann. Or again, many of the pioneers were priests, Anglican or Catholic, who looked in another direction. In the hills they found God's handiwork and among them tranquillity and the opportunity for adoration. It may not even be too fanciful to trace a link between their worship and that quiet acceptance of difficulty and hardship which characterized many of them: the willingness to sit out a night on the tops without sleeping equipment, and the ability even under these uncomfortable conditions to describe rapturously the beauty of peak and star.

A father to the mountain 'Weltanschauung' of many Englishmen of our own age was Leslie Stephen. A scholar, and formerly a priest, he looked in the mountains for everything that his religion had not given him. He 'climbed because he liked it', and if he could not discover the reason why he liked it, then he did not fret. His grandchildren are those who in their thousands leave factory and library to flood the mountain area nearest to their home; those who, without knowing why, fill every holiday that they have with mountain climbing, at home or abroad. In them has been born almost a new mysticism, that of writers like W. H. Murray. This no longer demands things from mountains, but is content to accept the experience as satisfying and allow it to lead them where it will. Thus Murray writes: 'Mercifully, it is in this very process of not understanding that one is allowed to understand much.' In their everyday life they will continue as before, normal and reasonable human beings. Holiday and their waking dreams they keep to themselves. For it is but a few bold spirits who have gone the whole length, with Eric Shipton, and given up their fortune to the 'tempting luxury' of an all-absorbing indulgence in exploration of the greatest ranges. Their way yet another literature lies. Just because of the wholeness of their passion, because of the daring and endurance of the deeds done, these few writers have brought to the fore and propagated the passionate enthusiasms of Martin Conway, Cecil Slingsby and Norman Collie. They would be the last to claim a place as littérateurs. But the simple narration of certain facts can have a Thucydidean sublimity. The future of mountain writing then may be with these, for the greater Himalaya are still virtually unclimbed. It may be, too, that such writing will no longer be a sideline of men normally engaged in other spheres, but an occupation itself fully satisfying.

The last word then is with the explorers in every region. An essay is permitted the whims of choice, for it is not a history. Robert Falcon Scott, to take an example, was not primarily interested in mountains themselves, but he was compelled to do much mountaineering to attain his objects. In the end, mountains played a larger part in his life than they have done in those of most of the writers described here. He made literature out of them, by a bare recital of his work on Antarctic hills and glaciers. Occasionally he spares a word for their beauty, and it is a word worth hearing. Mount Erebus, from the diaries, becomes an old and splendidly handsome friend. He too would have laid little claim to authorship. He wrote chiefly because he wanted to record accurately what his expeditions had done; he created literature and drama. Almost any schoolboy, asked who was the first man to reach the South Pole, would answer unhesitatingly 'Scott'. In part at least this is due to the 'literary' quality of the *Diary*, in part admittedly to the charm of Wilson's artistry, and to the dramatic end. Amundsen's *Journal*, by comparison, reads like a catalogue. Scott too therefore pointed a way to this writing that may be sustained in yet remoter fields: the literature of action, among surroundings that call upon the extremes of courage, of skill and of the capacity for companionship.

Heights and Depths in Dante

Perchè non sali il dilettoso monte
Ch'è principio e cagion di tutta gioia?

'O NORATE l'altissimo poeta!' Dante at least had seemed
to be affected by none of the human weaknesses.
Sternly he notes and reproves our most innocent follies,
curtly he consigns our wandering passions to the diverse
pits of his Inferno. Indeed we had almost passed him by,
as we skimmed the Middle Ages searching for the vestige
of a desire to climb mountains. Yet we pause, look again
at the *Divine Comedy*, and a new light is shed suddenly
upon him. Not only was he himself acquainted with mountains, but a certain view of their ultimate importance illu-
mines the texture of his whole poetic thought. He was a
man of the Middle Ages. His hills impend and seem about
to topple over on to his persons, so that it is not easy to
catch them in perspective. They are like the jumbled background to an early Florentine painting. But when the
human figures have been disentangled the hills remain
strangely present, behind, and Dante upon them. Looking
at them we feel suddenly that mountains and mountaineering may not be, as we feared, such a weakness in us. By

[23]

climbing these physical heights we are training ourselves for nothing less than the Purgatorial ascent. Dante is with us; and not only with us, but with us in the rôle of trembling and unwieldy novice, one who must be pushed and pulled by his guide, and indeed comes near to wrecking the whole expedition through Hell by his relapses into stark, terror-stricken immobility.

It is impossible to grant to Douglas Freshfield his claim that the Dante of the *Divine Comedy* was not the Dante of real life. If there was ever a writer who is the hero of his own story, he is here. Dante was no Shakespeare, to hide himself behind a multiplicity of characters. All his work, from the *Vita Nuova* onward, leaves the impression of his own burning personality. And his experiences on the slopes of Inferno and Purgatorio are no exception. They have the ring of reality. There is besides a fresh appreciation of hill beauty and an accuracy of observation which are quite new in literature, and which seem to spell intimate acquaintance. Dante too, wandering alone in winter, had remarked the early snow:

> *To the low light, wide circle of the shade,*
> *Poor man I come, and to the whitening hills.*[1]

No quotations torn from their context by Ruskin can wring that experience from him. Or in summer he had noted the peak that seems to look down on the water at its foot, bending as if to admire its own adornment:

> *And as a mountain looking on a lake*
> *Mirrors itself to see itself adorned,*
> *How fair it is with sweet young flowers and grass.*[2]

He had walked then among the Apennines or Alps at all seasons; it is not the biographies but the many references

---

[1] Al poco giorno ed al gran cerchio d'ombra
Son giunto, lasso! ed al bianchir de'colli (*Canzone* i).

[2] E come clivo in acqua di suo imo
Si specchia, quasi per vedersi adorno,
Quando è nell'erbe e neì fioretti opimo (*Par.* xxx, 109).

The Foot of Purgatory

in his poem which tell us that he had also climbed their steep sides, both alone and in company; he had climbed them, and brought into his writing, consciously or unconsciously, a view of life and death which they directly inspired.

.   .   .   .   .

The opening scene of the *Inferno* is set in a dark wood. After passing it, Dante attempts to climb a steep hill, toward which he had looked as we look from a forest up at the Alpine glow:

I looked on high, and saw its shoulders clad
Already with that glorious planet's ray
Which leads a man direct through every path.[3]

This hill produced the difficult expression that 'the stationary foot was always the lower'. There is a suggestion of a weary gait; it was almost too much for him to climb upward. Hereupon he is met by Virgil, who asks him why he does not continue the ascent of 'il dilettoso monte'. Aristocrat that he is, he is aware here of his own unworthiness and ashamed. He accepts Virgil's guidance, and the necessity first to climb down into the gigantic pot-hole which forms Hell, that he may purify himself to scramble out on the other side of the world to the ascent of Purgatory. The attempt on the hill then is abandoned. Down they plunge, to a vast blackness cut by such swirling blasts as hustle Francesca and the carnal sinners. Or they find themselves rock-climbing over the bastions that separate the various circles of punishment. Or they pause to watch the gluttons bathed in a true Cambrian mixture of rain and mud. At the end they make their perilous way over the hide of Lucifer, frozen firmly into the ice at the centre of the earth. This is a difficult climb; but they are at last

[3] Guardai in alto, e vidi le sue spalle
Vestite già de' raggi del pianeta
Che mena dritto altrui per ogni calle (*Inf.* i, 16).

ascending, on the other side, and on rock again, although it is still rock of some difficulty and rottenness:

> *It was no palace chimney where we were,*
> *But cranny carved by nature, rudely floored.*[4]

The *Inferno* then is arranged to portray the bleak and harsh aspects of mountain experience. These fit the fearful examples that Dante is to see, and inspire at the same time a cleverly graded crescendo of terror; at each circle the reader too is on his last legs. He can share the agony of Dante himself, who has by this time become almost a baggage, planted by Virgil (the careful guide) safely on each ledge while he goes on to explore the route. Glad they are to be off Lucifer and to see again the stars. But before that happens they have met with most of the difficulties faced by mountaineers. Twice at least they are cut off, as they descend, by an apparently bottomless pit. Dante, on the first occasion, loosens the cord girt round his waist, and they let it down (xvi, 109). Geryon swims up, and they are saved their difficulty. But what had been the purpose of the cord? To catch the ounce, whatever that symbolized, Dante tells us himself. Or equally well, the mountaineering commentators might claim, to attach him to Virgil, the guide. On another occasion they descend scree slopes, which like all scree slopes take an impish delight in moving when they are trodden upon:

> *that often stirred*
> *Under my feet, for feeling the new weight.*[5]

And at a crisis in their journey, when they are escaping from the demons whose pastime is the soaking of sinners in the pitch (like sheep that come slow to the dipping), Virgil is compelled to the expedient of seizing his pupil and rushing with him 'supino' down the steep mountain side. What

---

[4] Non era caminata di palagio
   Là 'v' eravam, ma natural burella
   Ch'avea mal suolo (*Inf.* xxxiv, 97).

[5]   che spesso moviensi
   Sotto i miei piedi per lo nuovo carco (*Inf.* xii, 29).

could 'supino' mean? Perhaps that he leant back to the slope, taking it with straight legs as only a very strong runner can do.

But the most perilous rock passage of all is that in canto xxiv, when the explorers are making their way from one pit of Malebolge to the next. Informed of the route, but perplexed as to its exact line, they are confronted by a huge rock obstacle. This they assault, using combined tactics.

> *As one who works and estimates ahead,*
> *Who seems he always would provide before,*
> *So he, raising me up toward the crest*
> *Of the one splinter, looked up to the next*
> *And said: 'Grasp that one after, but try first*
> *If it be firm to bear you as you climb.'*
> *This was no way for one clad in a cope,*
> *For we with pain, he light and I propelled,*
> *Were able to mount up from ledge to ledge.*
> *And were it not that rather on this side*
> *Than on the other the hill's slope was short,*
> *Of him I know not,—I had surely failed.*[6]

Here is rich store of material: the extreme difficulty and rottenness of the rock; Virgil's promptness and Dante's inability (which is remarkable even on supernatural rocks; or perhaps he did not like to show greater competence than his age would have considered reasonable); and yet his

[6] E come quei che adopera ed estima,
Che sempre par che innanzi si provveggia,
Così, levando me su ver la cima

D'un ronchion, avvisava un'altra scheggia,
Dicendo: "Sopra quella poi t'aggrappa;
Ma tenta pria s'è tal ch'ella ti reggia."

Non era via da vestito di cappa,
Chè noi a pena, ei lieve ed io sospinto,
Potevam su montar di chiappa in chiappa.

E se non fosse che da quel precinto,
Più che dall' altro, era la costa corta,
Non so di lui, ma io sarei ben vinto (*Inf.* xxiv, 25-36).

willingness, though nearly beat, to go on when urged, showing himself 'outwardly better furnished with breath than I felt'. A few lines later the way becomes harder again but he struggles on, as many and many have done since, trying not to show his weakness upon a hillside to a stronger companion. It is a common trick to talk, so as not to appear breathless:

Talking I climbed and would not appear weak.[7]

At last they win their goal. But we could multiply indefinitely instances of the rugged and terrible in his mountains: the mist that magnifies the abyss of the last descent (xxxi); the ground frost that is sister to snow (xxiv, 4); the rock splinters where hands must aid feet (xxvi), or the rough ground where even the goats would find difficulty (xix, 131); and the ice which makes the sinners' faces 'doglike with cold'. Assuredly his novitiate was roughly passed. And small wonder that, at the beginning of the descent, he mistakes the pallor of Virgil's look for fear. He is assured however that it is pity only for the condemned that has changed his guide's colour.

.   .   .   .   .

Purgatory, from the very opening lines of the first canto, breathes a very different atmosphere. It inspires confidence because it is a mountain, not a hole. The human spirit has had its fill of horror, of damp mists and pits that appear bottomless. Purged, it is prepared to begin the upward climb that leads finally to Heaven. But the way, like the way up our physical Alps, is steep and winding. Of all comers the travellers must ask 'which way to go', and how often have we too exclaimed, when confronted by insuperable rock:

Who knows now on which side the path may mount,
Whereby, unhelped of wings, a man can climb?[8]

[7] Parlando andava per non parer fievole (*Inf.* xxiv, 64).
[8] Or chi sa da qual man la costa cala . . .
    Sì che possa salir chi va senz'ala? (*Pur.* iii, 52).

This question is asked of the first rise from the seashore. The mountain springs up in a cliff steep as the landslide between Lerici and Turbia, cut by a gap narrow as the gap in a hedge which a hedger makes. Up this all must go, using hands as well as feet, until they are on the open hillside which is still, as Dante scrupulously notes, set at an angle of more than 45 degrees. He seems to us to be estimating with that happy abandon common to all early travellers among the Alps. We have read so often such passages: 'Above us the cliff rose vertical. Below, the ice slope plunged at an angle of sixty degrees, to end in the overhang which we had just surmounted.' Thus the Victorian pioneers, for even so does hyperbole overtake us all. Human too, and symbolic, is Dante's desire to rest on a ledge and to look back,

Since looking back must delight any man.[9]

Here he asks Virgil how long the way will be, for he is tired and the summit is far out of sight. The poet who has struggled through the morass of the Infernal hole is inevitably wearied by the beginnings of a real peak. It is pleasanter to sit and look back than to go on. Naturally with training (as Virgil explains), and with the feeling of height won, the way becomes easier and the climbing more pleasurable. Sluggards only are vanquished—and they pass Belacqua, the fine craftsman, too idle to climb farther. Dante himself, as he goes on, presses with an ever-increasing eagerness towards the top. It is at last Piccarda who shows him, in the lowest sphere of Heaven, that it is not really such ambition, but content with the heights permitted, that makes for true happiness. But that is in the realm of the stars.

As they proceed up the mountain their pace quickens and he assumes that the going will be faster still during the night. He had possibly walked on mountain snow, and knew how an early start gives the hard, quick surface. But

[9] Chè suole a riguardar giovare altrui (*Pur.* iv, 54).

Sordello explains that it is impossible to move upward at night, and they traverse down into the Valley of the Kings. Here they sleep. The problem now before him is to give an impression of loftiness to Purgatory such as will strike his readers with its sublimity. Details of their innocent and not very speedy scrambling towards a summit so far indicate a very modest peak. Therefore during the first night he has himself transported in sleep by Lucia up to the entrance of Purgatory proper. Imagination magnifies the distance. At dawn, then, he awakens before the gateway. The two pass it, and enter a narrow passage above. He is careful to recount the difficulties and labour of this ascent, in the awful 'curving crack' above the gateway. Non-mountaineering commentators have been so rash as to believe that the rock itself is supposed to be bending and swaying. Those fortunate ones who have looked at the buttresses of Lliwedd on Snowdon will know better. Then between the circles, and on the seventh circle between the fire and the cornice overhanging space, there are further perils. Virgil is 'guide' and 'leader' as often as 'sweet father', although significantly enough, the farther they go the less Dante feels that he has need of him.

Finally at the summit, which in contradiction to Alpine tops is the green and luscious Earthly Paradise, he dispenses with a guide altogether. Trained to the heights and master of his first trembling, the aspirant needs no further human support. The divine Beatrice, the woman, takes Virgil's place, to carry him from the hills and to show him the way among the stars. Purgatory then is the height of human endeavour, as the Inferno was its depth; and it is a mountain, since mountains are the highest it is given us on earth to reach. So running through the texture are the similes which go to heighten such an impression. Some are of familiar experience, like the metaphor of the mountaineer (if Ruskin will allow it to be

[30]

such, and not merely a taunt at the crude mountain
dweller):

> *Not otherwise the mountaineer confused*
> *Stands stupid, gazing round in dumb surprise,*
> *When to the city, rough and wild, he comes.*[10]

So do we too descend from the snows, to trudge uncouth
and unshaven into the glitter of the valley towns. But for
the most part he chooses beauty and strength in his pictures: the sun which the climber in the Alps sees slowly
conquering the mist, dim at first but radiant as it gains
strength (xxx, 22); Beatrice, whom he can compare only
to the rosy, glowing beauty of mountain sunrise (xxvii, 1);
and the 'green shade' of clouds that pass over the hills,
above their cold streams (xxxiii, 110).

.   .   .   .   .

The *Paradiso* contains less immediate reference to hills.
But the *Paradiso* is necessary to complete the mountain
picture. At the beginning Dante claims that he has already
won the first peak of Parnassus; as a poet, he is now ambi-
tious for the second (i, 17), far different from the timid
traveller on the earliest hill. It seems that the heights
climbed, if they were worth the climbing, were worth it to
some end, that of the eternal Heavens. The Earthly Paradise
itself is not enough. It fits a man only, makes him 'Pure
and disposed to climb up to the stars'. Therefore the poet,
now almost over-satisfied with his own qualifications, asks
Piccarda, a lady whom he meets in the lowest sphere of the
moon, why she does not try to rise higher, as would seem
natural if she wishes to attain fuller vision. Her answer,
that in His Will is our peace, restores proportion. Belacqua,
and Dante himself, had longed to stay sitting near the bottom of Purgatory. Theirs was idleness. But she, who is in
Heaven, knows that her own low place in it is a part of the

[10] Non altrimenti stupido si turba
    Lo montanaro, e rimirando ammuta
    Quando rozzo e selvatico s'inurba (*Pur.* xxvi, 67).

[31]

Divine Plan, and she is acquiescent. Not for sluggishness of soul, but because it is God's pleasure and therefore hers, does she remain content where she is, knowing as they did not know that this is the highest she can claim.

Herein lies the lesson of the *Paradiso*. Dante has conquered sloth, he has climbed the hill. He is now told that climbing high is not of itself meritorious. What is meritorious is to achieve the best allowed and to rest content in that; just as we who climb the mountains of earth, and who have looked for the highest in physical height, come to realize that it is not height which matters, but happiness, at whatever level it be granted. And if we must descend to the foothills, if war or disability keeps us from the summits, such descent is spiritually no descending, provided our content in the hills be the same.

There are some passages in the *Paradiso* which directly recall mountains: the sound of chill winds that blow, the picture of hermitages set upon rocks so high 'that even the thunder sounds beneath the rock', and bird's-eye views of

The little plot for which we wax so fierce (xxii, 151).

But Dante is not content, like Piccarda, to remain below. Having pointed the moral he must needs mount himself to the highest sphere of Heaven, and leave her to her peace. He is destined to see the Trinity, to be wrapped in the unutterable peace towards which the hill of Purgatory merely pointed. Let us only hope that he did not altogether forget the peak he had climbed and his other wanderings, if such can be inferred, in the Alps and Apennines. It was left to Petrarch to make the first recorded ascent whose object was simply the climb and the view. But Dante before him, though his picture is the medieval one and still confused, had interpreted them symbolically, so that they assume a meaning in our mortal life. And if he did not neglect his hill experience, but was rather grateful for it in the bliss of Paradise, we in turn should give thanks. For they have, across the years, shown us some more familiar side of the poet we had feared unapproachable, and given new colour to a poem once a terrible and unearthly mosaic in our imagination. They have in Dante marked the middle land through which he travelled to find Beatrice. They are the symbol of a mortal and physical medium, but a medium between temporary trials and despairs, and the eternal stars towards which they rise.

Petrarca Alpinista

Solo e pensoso i più deserti campi
Vo misurando a passi tardi e lenti.

PETRARCH has long been reputed the first mountaineer in the modern sense. He was a person who went out to climb a mountain with no apparent purpose beyond reaching the summit and seeing what was to be seen from it. It is true that his claim to be called father of mountaineering rests on the slender foundation of a single climb. But we may see, looking at what was in his day a startling enough ascent, an attitude of mind which bears all the seeds of our modern urge for mountain exploration, and our capacity for mountain worship.

It was in 1336 that he reached the summit of Mont Ventoux, a peak of 6,427 feet, in the neighbourhood of Avignon. He had known it a long time and had long wanted to climb it, as we so often want to climb the familiar hills which have looked down on our youth. He did the climb on April 26th, after a period of preparation, and he described it in a letter to Dionisio Roberti of Borgo San Sepolcro. This letter he wrote while the mood of his moments at the summit was still upon him. The party

[35]

arrived late and tired, and he withdrew at once to write, while supper was being prepared. In the letter he appears before us, receiving the mountain torch from Dante, and handing it across the lost centuries to the pioneers who followed after the Romantic Movement. But this was not all. For this one letter could not have been written by a man out of sympathy with the wider call of natural things. When we have considered it, we shall find that all his poetry was in tune with his reflections on the summit of Mont Ventoux, that his thoughts about Laura herself were coloured by the flowers and hills that formed a background to her charms. But we must first inspect the letter.

Petrarch approached his mountain not only as a poet and admirer from afar. He was peculiarly modern. He had advanced even beyond our nineteenth-century Romantics, who sang of Mont Blanc 'still, snowy and serene', but were not forward when it came to climbing over laborious summits. Petrarch came as a humanist, one interested in these mountains in proportion as they affected him, the microscopically small but nevertheless important human being. He was the humane man, not concerned to exalt them into the sublime and terrible figures of Shelley's poem, but to climb them because they attracted him and then, if he felt humble, to feel so before his own thoughts at the power of God who had created both himself and them.

It has been at all times the mystics, scholars and poets who have climbed most readily into the hills for spiritual refreshment. They have liked at the same time to exhaust their bodies by physical exertion. The farmers and road-builders have felt no need for such escape, nor have they enjoyed the leisure for lengthy reflection. Very often too these pioneers have been persons unused to the manual tasks, who have worked upon this one liking until it was strong enough to yield a satisfying contact with the earthy things otherwise denied to them. Petrarch was above all else a scholar and a poet. It is true that he had toiled at

times with his hands. His landscape-gardening labours at
Vaucluse and his draughtsmanship show this. But he would
have admitted that in manual dexterity he fell far short of
his brother Gherardo, whom he chose to be companion on
this venture. He set about the choosing with as much care
as the leader of a Himalayan expedition. The one man went
too fast, the next too slow; this candidate was too hasty in
judgement, the next too stolid. Each of them he weighed
and found wanting, until his mind's eye lighted upon the
faithful Gherardo. Here was a person perhaps a little slow
by temperament but utterly reliable and a man of great
physical strength. He too had been at grips with an affair
of the heart, and was ready now to be distracted and at the
same time flattered by an invitation from his famous
brother. Gherardo then it should be.

It was characteristic of Petrarch's serious approach that
he planned a day of rest to be spent at Malaucène before
the assault. It was April 25th, and they passed it looking up
at the 'precipitous and inaccessible mass of rocky ground'
which they were to climb. On the 26th they made the ascent,
starting early. The stages of the climb are worth noting,
for they correspond with those of so many another expedition since Petrarch's day. First they meet the shepherd,
who warns them that the hill is dangerous and attempts to
dissuade them from the attempt. He is a gloomy prophet
whom we later climbers have met often enough. The hill is
indeed, he says, almost impossible of ascent, and he points
a forbidding finger up at the perilous slopes. Then they come
to a rocky ridge up which the brother mounts direct. But
Petrarch, the man of imagination, is tempted by a path which
looks longer but which he hopes will prove easier. The first
time it is a slanting gangway which leads him off the ridge:

Whilst my brother was seeking short cuts over the steepest parts
of the mountain, I more warily kept below, and when he pointed out
the path to me, I answered that I hoped to find an easier access, and
that I more willingly went round in order to advance on more level
ground. But whilst I was alleging this excuse for my laziness, he got

far above me, and I was wandering in the gullies of the mountain, where my path was far from being easier, so that the way lengthened and my useless labour became more and more irksome. As it was too late to repent of my error, I determined to go straight up, and I at last rejoined my brother, whom I had lost from sight, and who had been quietly resting on a rock, after much toil and anxiety, so that we started again together. The same thing however happened again and again in a few hours. The truth was that I was shirking the trouble of climbing; but human ingenuity cannot alter the nature of things, nor is it possible for anything corporeal to reach the heights by going downward. . . . I could not help apostrophizing myself in the following words: 'The very thing which has happened to thee in the ascent of this mountain happens to thee and to many of those who seek to arrive at final beatitude. . . .'

Both the act of evasion and the reflection were characteristic; for the simpler Gherardo had no doubts or difficulties but climbed straight up, to wait patiently at the top. But Petrarch's weak yielding is followed by a flood of gloomy moralizing upon his own frailty. 'What holds thee back, but the more level path along earthly and mean delights?' and 'as the ascent, so also is life'.

But they are up at last, and on the summit they are greeted by the astonishing view of the Alps. Now Petrarch, no less than the Victorian pioneers after him, felt it necessary to describe this view, in order perhaps to give an aesthetic justification to his ascent. The description of the summit, as of the climb, proceeds in stages, from the outward scene to the inner reflection. At first it is the sudden glory of the Alps which impresses him for itself alone. He experiences that wonderful sensation of self-oblivion which all mountaineers have known before the best of views. But he cannot rest there. He is a westerner, and the scene is significant for him just because it is related to his own conception of God and love. He reflects: beyond those peaks lies Italy, and it is ten years now since my departure, at the end of my studies, from Bologna. Then, turning his thoughts more and more inward, he ponders over other dates in his life. It is three years since the passion for the beloved Laura first met with a challenge. There has been improvement, certainly, in himself, even if there is much still to lament. How happy he would be if he could die, another ten years hence, with yet another advance to his credit!

The feeling of inadequacy before God's Nature, with the sensation sweetly mingling of hope that these things may with time be improved, leads him to turn to his consolation in all difficulty: the *Confessions of Saint Augustine*. He opens the book at random, to see what the chance passage may contain. He is struck with astonishment as he reads aloud: 'Men go abroad to admire the heights of mountains and the long winding courses of rivers, the compass of the Ocean and the courses of the stars, and themselves they forget.' The appropriateness of this passage amazes him. But it is unlikely that the lesson has really struck home. It is the old lesson, that men must forget themselves, if they are fully to appreciate their surroundings; before the high mountains and the deep rivers which are, as it were, huge half-personalities interposed between them and the Divine, they must lose themselves in adoration. It is these greater creatures which assist our worship of that Power beyond, which is too vast for comprehension. This of course is akin to Buddhist doctrine; we escape the Round of Activity which is Karma, by successfully forgetting or annihilating ourselves. But Petrarch's own reaction to the view, after his earliest wonder, has been to turn evermore inward and to consider private failings and hopes in relation to the scene which aroused his earlier sensations. Here again, just because he is a humanist, he is drawn back at once to the human things. God Himself the Creator is important, not only because He created these wonderful Alps but because He created man, and in particular Petrarch. It is appropriate then that upon this summit he should propose to himself to write the only letter written during Laura's lifetime which refers directly to his passion for her. The associations of her name and his are linked with hill places.

They begin the descent, for Petrarch refuses fully to

satisfy his brother's curiosity about the passage he has just read. They look back every now and then at the summit receding into the distance. Petrarch is impressed, not by the greatness of that summit (nor even of their achievement), but by its smallness in comparison with the heights of human thought. When therefore they have reached the inn he retires to write the letter to his mentor which shall describe the adventure and seek advice. 'Give up one hour to listening to the doings of one of my days.'

Petrarch was a restless creature at that time, discontented with the city life at Avignon, with the court and with his own efforts to overcome his love for Laura. At the age of twenty-five he had set off on a journey to Belgium and other parts of the Continent, which certainly broadened his mind and interested him in personalities as well as letters. But he was still not content. He came back ready to find in natural things a foil for his dissatisfied mood. He has been criticized for writing subjectively, for introducing into his descriptions of scenery his own gloomy religious perplexities. But such was the character of the man, and as such it must be accepted; it was the character also of the Renaissance on which he set his stamp. A more weighty criticism would be that his mountain enthusiasm was no more than a brief flash, that he never returned to climb the same peak again or to attempt some other of the many that surrounded him, even though he chose a later home among the Euganean hills. Part of the answer has already been indicated. He was the humanist, he set man at the centre of his Universe and was almost surprised into awe when he found himself on a summit. It may be true indeed that the whole Renaissance so steeped itself in his humanism that only men scientifically interested, like Leonardo da Vinci, could wish to climb mountains—for much the same reasons as de Saussure 300 years later. Petrarch perhaps feared too that familiarity might vulgarize the sublimities which he had witnessed. The experience had been so tremendous that

The Valley of Vancluse and the Slopes of Mont Ventaux

it could not be repeated. Better to leave it as a memory. But its atmosphere is breathed already into his poetry, and to his poetry we shall look, to make sure that the vision upon Mont Ventoux was no isolated happening in his life.

The recurrent theme of the poems is Laura, and we find as we look through them a natural and pleasing background to her charms in the hills and valleys against which she is set. Petrarch, it must be admitted, did at times subscribe to the common view of the Middle Ages that mountains were large obstacles; barriers useful or unpleasant depending upon which way you looked at them. In the patriotic canzone 'to Italy' he summons the Italians to unite against the foreigner. It is then that he cries, in medieval vein:

Nature served well our state
Then, when she set the shield
Of the Alps between us and the Germans' rage.[11]

But the mountains and other facets of Nature were far more for him even from the beginning than mere walls to be passed without delight. In the first place they represented associations with Laura. The very beautiful fourteenth canzone is woven around the grass bank on which he had first seen her. Such a relationship called to mind between loved person and natural feature, familiar to us now, was almost a novelty in that age.

This grass from that time has so pleased my heart
That here, and nowhere else, I can find peace.[12]

For surely, where Laura had been, there was Paradise. Where the Rhône came tumbling from his rock ravines it must be to wash her feet (173rd sonnet); where the 'sweet hills' of Vaucluse rose to surround him with their peace (174th sonnet), it was with memories of her alone that they filled him. Thus in the poems too he strikes the new note of

[11] Ben provide Natura al nostro stato
quando de l'Alpi schermo
pose fra noi e la tedesca rabbia.

[12] Da indi in qua mi piace
quest'erba sì, ch'altrove non ho pace.

individual man, or of man and woman, seen against a background of Nature. It was a note hinted already, but not fully
worked upon, by Dante. From his Nature he draws the quality that links her with persons, and himself with the beloved.
So had the Alps, seen from Mont Ventoux, been associated
for him with his dear native Italy beyond. So it is now

Beyond those Alps,
There, where the sky shines more serene and glad

that he looks, for beyond his symbolic Alps Laura is wait-
ing for him, and there alone he can find peace.

But natural scenery had much to it besides association. It
was sympathetic to intellectual effort, for instance. In the
sonnet to Giacomo Colonna

No palace here, no theatre or arcade,
But in their place a pine, or beech, or fir,
Between the green grass and the fair hill near
(*Whence as we rhyming come our steps are stayed*)
Raises our thoughts from earth and points them high.[13]

Or more commonly their wild places are the sympathetic
recipients of secrets which no man must know. Two poems
in particular illustrate this mood. In the eighteenth sonnet,
among the loveliest of all, it is stated explicitly. He goes
'solo e pensoso' where the wildest regions are, because he
does not wish to expose to human eye the passion that
consumes him. It does not matter if the mountains know,
indeed they can be his comforters, for they share much of
his history already:

So that I do believe that hills and shores,
Rivers and woods now know what is the stuff
That knits my life,—all I have kept from men.[14]

[13] Qui non palazzi, non teatro o loggia,
Ma'n lor vece un abete un faggio un pino
Tra l'erba verde e'l bel monte vicino,
Onde si scende poetando e poggia,
Levan di terra al ciel nostr' intelletto.

[14] Sì ch'io mi credo omai che monti e piagge
e fiumi e silve sappian di che tempre
sia la mia vita, ch'è celata altrui.

Even the winds that blow across the ravines are an accompaniment to his agonized thought. This idea is developed further in the seventeenth canzone, the most significant of the 'Nature' poems. Here he is out quite deliberately to fret himself, beguiling the time while he is far from Laura. He is restless and the hills draw him to them. They supply comfort or at least an accordance of mood.

> *Through the high mountains and harsh woods I find*
> *A little ease.*[15]

A few lines later he is more explicit:

> *Up where no overshadowing mountain stands,*
> *Towards the greatest and the loftiest peak*
> *A fiery longing ever draws me on.*[16]

It is the same longing that drew him to the top of Mont Ventoux, and we must ask again what it represents. May it be here the need of something, of some 'height', to replace the perfection of Laura who has been herself associated with these physical mountains? At least he may wish to substitute an object that shall appease his desire for her. In the light of modern psychology his experience is full of meaning. For when he reaches his summit, or when he stops to rest 'under the shadow of tall pine or hill', then the scenery recalls her to him again and he weeps, filled with the old longing for what he can never possess.

Petrarch then was beginning to sort out the mosaic left by the Middle Ages. The medieval picture had been 'all foreground with no perspective', a rich pageant of persons behind whom the hills reared their fantastic walls. It is a scene bewildering in detail because the eye cannot focus upon the different objects, heaped and tangled together. He extracted from that scene the individual human. Often he would liken that human to the inanimate, as when

[15] Per alti monti e per aspre silve trovo
Qualche riposo.
[16] Ove d'altra montagna ombra non tocchi,
verso 'l maggiore e'l più spedito giogo
tirar mi suol un desiderio intenso.

Laura's heart is a frozen thing, as impenetrable as Dante's 'donna di pietra'. But it is ultimately the living and breathing person whom he puts forward as valuable, with Nature in her due perspective some way behind and above, to represent the other manifestations of God's power. In this matter we of the west have taken a very different course from that of the eastern sages, and it is Petrarch who has helped greatly to stamp our individuality upon us. For it is only in rare and unguarded moments that we forget ourselves before that power, and we practise in our daily lives something very different from that Meditation which would lose us in self-oblivion or Nirvana. We prefer action, we return from the hills to assert ourselves. Or we are to be found ever wandering, like Petrarch, striving, after it all, to climb some peak 'touched by the shadow of no higher summit'.

Note to Chapter Two

There is a considerable bibliography on the Alpinism of Petrarch (as also, of course, of Dante). Most of this is in the form of articles and essays in Alpine and other journals, and for a fuller list of Petrarchian studies it is worth examining the list of Paul Guiton in the *Rivista del Club Alpino Italiano*, 1937. There is besides the well-known essay by Carducci, *Il Petrarca Alpinista*, and a thorough study of the poet's outlook on Nature in Zumbini's *Studi sul Petrarca*. Zumbini believes Petrarch's letter to be sincere and revealing, and that the time of his life at which it was written was an imaginative climax in his thought. His view of Petrarch's Nature feeling very much corresponds with that indicated in these pages: that he was not one of those poets who take their Nature the primitive, almost subconscious, way as part with the air they breathe. He looked at her as a human, and asked himself with what human persons or what piece of human history he might associate her in order to point the moral of her beauty.

Another book of interest, but in lighter vein, is *Curiosità Dantesche* by Paolo Bellezza. In the section 'Dante e l'alpinismo' he affirms that Dante and Petrarch were scarcely real mountaineers—indeed how could they so far have outrun their age? And of course they would not have found their way into the most modest of modern climbing fraternities. But indeed their interest lies for us just in that part of them which succeeded in outstripping their age at all. We do not expect them to be competent Alpinists, in an age when nobody had heard of Alpinism.

More recently a book has been written by Professor G. Billanovich which argues that 'The letter in which Petrach described his climbing of Mont Ventoux was written fairly late, about 1352, and that it was composed by him not to be sent but merely as a literary exercise' (*Petrarca Letterato*, vol. i, 'Lo Scrittoio del Petrarca', 1947). This is a novel and in some ways disturbing view. There is much to be said for it: Petrarch's lack of interest in any other ascents, the exceptional absence of snow on the mountain at the end of April, the elaborate coincidence recorded on the summit. At the same time the letter breathes so distinctly a real mountain experience that it is difficult to believe that it does not describe one. There are so many small human touches known to few but mountaineers. And yet, of course, even if the whole climb was no more a fact than the ascent of Purgatory, it would make little difference to Petrarch either as mountain humanist or mountaineer psychologist. It is the progress of the mind rather than the physical steps that we count.

The Sentimentality of Rousseau

O Nature! O ma mère! Me voici sous ta seule garde!

JEAN-JACQUES ROUSSEAU would be surprised to find himself in a portrait gallery of the mountain prophets. The man's very physique, his detractors would remark, rules him out. As a biographer writes, 'He had corns which forced him to walk on his heels. He had dangling arms and was so heavy on his feet that he could not jump over a gutter.' He had been the despair of the fencing-master, in the days when Madame de Warens thought that it would be good for his health to take exercise. Later, at Motiers in 1762, it was only because he must do something active to rid his system of its poisons that he could be induced into the cold out-of-doors to chop wood. Left to himself, he tells us, during his sojourn on the island of St Pierre, he would take a boat in which he would lie and dream through a 'soothing idleness'. But apart from his natural bent, he was early afflicted with a bladder disease which made any active exertion painful and finally impossible. Certainly, we might think, Rousseau is the last person to inspire us in our search for mountain personalities.

[47]

Yet as is well known, his influence on the growth of feeling for Nature and mountains was enormous. Was he not hailed as the fountain-head and father of mountain sensibility, and did not the visitors flock to the hills of Valais and of Vaud which he had celebrated? Of course it is true that he would have been capable of practising and preaching two very different creeds. He could write his *Émile* about education and leave his own children at the orphanage door. He might therefore have exhorted the young to the heights down which he felt too giddy to look, while he himself lay in his boat at the bottom. But this is not altogether his case. He did so lie, certainly, but he did a little more; he also walked. Indeed he found that he must walk, both to compose his writings and even to be truly himself. Further, he developed the doctrine that mountains were not only a beautiful part of Nature, as many people, especially in England, were beginning to see already, but that they were essential. They had their niche in that natural cathedral in which alone he would consent to walk and worship. Rousseau contemplated and adored. It was left for the Wordsworths and the pioneers of last century to go restlessly seeking what more active part a man could play in that mountain life. But we may first ask what he himself admired in those hills of his.

From the peaks themselves, as we would expect, he requires no very stark sublimity. When he crossed the Channel to England in 1766 he did not enjoy the experience and he certainly did not appreciate the sea. 'The sea appeals to virile natures.' Rousseau's nature was not virile, and besides he was a man of the eighteenth century. He would indeed have been in advance of that century had he really enjoyed the wild places for their own sake. M. Mornet argues that his temperament was not even that of the Romantic, although he sowed the seeds of Romanticism. He could not stomach Nature too raw, and he did not care to expose himself to her fury. 'He loved his Nature smiling

[48]

The House and Ridge at Les Charmettes

and peaceful.' As he wrote himself in his *Correspondence*: 'I know of no abode that is sad and ugly provided that it has grass. But if there is nothing but sand and bare rocks—say no more about it.' Naturally then from what we have seen of his figure and his habits, he did not go to the heights for the austerities. He 'always loved Nature for her peaceful, smiling moods rather than for her grandeur and the magnificence of her convulsions. Though he speaks of having loved rocks, waterfalls and rushing streams, the descriptive passages in his works are chiefly of meadows and woods.' The words 'I fling myself at the rocks' make us smile in the mouth of Saint-Preux, hero of *La Nouvelle Héloïse*, who may be taken at many points to represent Rousseau himself. What he loved most, and what he set the immediate fashion for loving in all but the sternest souls, was what Saint-Preux saw of especial beauty in the Valais: 'That astonishing mixture of wild and cultivated Nature.' It was the contrast of these two in a small space that attracted him in the island of St Pierre on the Lake of Bienne, where he had spent four happy months after the persecutions of Motiers. This means that the mountains are allowed to be as high and as steep as they please, provided that they look down upon fields and charming woods. For he could go into ecstasies at a word over a flower or a swallow, but he found difficult the rapturous description of a naked precipice or ravine. The 'horribles beautés' made fashionable by Young and the 'jardins anglais' were not for him.

What this 'homme sensible' then sought in mountain scenery was order, contrast, harmony, a certain rhythm that seemed to coincide with his own rhythm as he walked. For if he was not able or willing to climb the steep heights, at least he was always to be found walking among them when he was well enough to walk and receive their inspiration. The key to his later influence lies here. The following generations felt that he had been 'in touch' with the genius

D

of the valleys and wooded slopes in some special way; hence, they suspected, with the cliffs and ridges too. The gentle height above Les Charmettes was his ideal medium, a mountain ridge, if it could be so described, which allowed him to dream peacefully and threatened him with no natural extravagances. The summit has a prospect of steep cliffs and fine heights, but they are at a safe distance. And what good things do the mountains offer, Rousseau would have said, if it be not peace and a sense of security? On the road from Lyons to Chambéry there is a wall, and below the wall a cliff. Jean-Jacques felt giddy when he looked down from a height, but he enjoyed the sensation, provided he was in a safe position. 'The road is bordered with a parapet to prevent accidents. This meant that I could look down and experience vertigo just as I pleased; for the odd thing about my liking for precipitous places is that they make me giddy, and I enjoy this giddiness greatly, provided that I am safely placed.' A sense of security then was one of his demands from the mountains.

At the same time he liked to feel that he was very near the perilous edge. On this occasion, as if to emphasize both these sensations, off he goes to find boulders which he can 'trundle' down the cliff, for the pleasure of seeing them smash to pieces at the bottom. This pleasure in seeing destruction, with the attendant requisite of safety for himself, suggests the next consideration—the relation between man and mountain. Security meant for him security from the possible persecutions of fellow men. Even as a youth wandering without fortune but free of care to Turin he had found 'in the mountains, bowls of milk and cream, an enchanting idleness, peace, simplicity, the pleasure of wandering without knowing where'. In old age, extravagant and persecuted, he states explicitly in the *Rêveries* that he fled to Nature to escape. He recalls his horror, when he thought he had discovered a secluded Alpine valley, at finding that a large industrial establishment had preceded him. Nature then was to be a mother and protectress, and the mountains were the fortress of her purity. 'It seems that in raising oneself above the dwellings of men one leaves behind all low and earthly sentiments.'

It is hardly surprising that the idea of the comparative longevity and solidity of the hills should link itself with these comforting qualities. The hills represent a lasting and stable feature of this world, going on where men with their pettiness and persecutions fade and die. Saint-Preux's self-control is taxed almost beyond measure when he returns to the wild spot which he had visited in earlier days with Julie. He sees the same Alps, and remembers that those glaciers 'which are ever growing, have covered them since the beginning of the world'. For since mountains are a creation more enduring than ourselves, they provide these landscapes which cause us to remember ourselves as we were at other times, to recall earlier and happier days or the shape of a loved person. 'When I climbed over a difficult piece of rock, I seemed to see you pass it with the lightness of a fawn.' 'Everything recalled you to me in this peaceful abode.' Such sentiment, and we might say such sentimentality, abounds in the first part of *La Nouvelle Héloïse*. It is one of the duties of Nature to provide the meeting-places whose memories are the subject of Rousseau's 'sweetest dreams'.

The rôle of Nature then is that of mother to son, although she appears at times almost in the guise of an elder and sympathetic sister. If the mood of the man be stormy, it is fitting that Nature's mood should be stormy too. Saint-Preux writes to Julie: 'Perhaps the place where I am contributes to this melancholy. It is grim and gloomy; it is all the more in accord with the state of my heart, and I could not endure so patiently in a more agreeable abode. A line of barren rocks borders the hillside and surrounds my dwelling, a spot which the winter has made even more terrible.' He has gone out to find his peace in the wildest natural surroundings. He was perhaps braver than the Rousseau who loved his Nature 'smiling and peaceful', and who did not enjoy tempests. He is also able to voice some of the sterner sentiments which his creator never quite had the confidence to utter in the first person. He can sympathize with Nature at her most severe. But in whatever form she appears, Rousseau himself cannot ultimately escape her. He never thinks of man without that link with the landscape behind him; if he has no mountains or countryside at his beck, he must fill his background with the extravagance of palaces, and in them he is not really happy. He never found content near Paris. For here is his religion. On the ridge behind Les Charmettes he would mount each morning to say his 'prayer'. This was more a meditation than a prayer, and it could not be said in a room. 'This act consisted more of contemplation and admiration than of demands.' Indeed it was an act of worship in the deepest sense, for it was an attempt made part consciously, part unconsciously, to lose identity in a greater and worthier whole. Thus he will often, especially in the *Rêveries*, start on an accurate description of a scene; gradually, from being objective, the description links itself with the describer, the man. Then the man himself seems to disappear in the reverie, in contemplation of what is around him. The meadows and woods and ridges provide a 'cradling of the spirit'. All is peaceful, holy, comforting. The final stage of the Jean-Jacques religion is a nirvana in which he dissolves; he can dream and adore but not think. He is the most Oriental of sages.

It must be quite clear by now why he was no very active mountaineer. He was never interested, for obvious reasons, in physical movement for its effect on his body, but only for the dreams which it allowed. Arrived at the Hermitage 'I began by making arrangements for my walks', and this even before he thought of arranging his books or hours of study. Those walks we have said took him among the hills and hill people. But just as he will start with an accurate description of a scene, to wander off into random impressions of the effect produced upon himself, so with the country dwellers whose cause he claims to espouse we are tempted to suspect that he is not really interested. At any rate he is not interested in them as persons, but only as supporters of his Theory—that civilization corrupts, and that the simple land dwellers are the happiest. He will start by describing, then launch into a dissertation on their merits or grievances. He seems to see in them no more than the victims of injustice or the paragons of primitive virtue. When he first left Geneva in 1728 he very soon tired of the company of the hospitable peasants who gave him food and shelter—and made his way to the town of Confignon. On his return at a later date to Madame de Warens he was excited by the peasant who gave him bread and milk only, and then finding that he was not after all a tax collector provided a real dinner. But he was struck with him not as a person, nor does he in fact describe his character, but as the abstract type of the victim of injustice. There are few memorable country personages among his pages, no leech-gatherers or gipsies such as hold us in Dorothy Wordsworth's *Journal*. The peasants of the Valais impress Saint-Preux rather for their collective quality as happy mountain farmers than as individuals. Indeed so out of touch is Rousseau at times that he is surprised when the country folk are not impressed as he is by the beauties that surround them. 'Why is their soul not raised in an ecstasy to the author of the marvels which strike their senses?' The answer is simple to anyone who has worked on a farm, but it is one that he will never understand. For the truth is that he was using men without consulting them first. Rocks were savage and therefore noble because primitive peoples and mountain dwellers were savage and noble. They were thus a convenient prop to his theory of the corruption of mankind, and as such he used them mercilessly. He never paused to study them in the interested, unasking spirit of de Saussure.

Here then is the anomaly of one himself unfriendly to the idea of climbing steep places, who yet is in some sense the father of those who later were eager to explore them. In part this is because he came at the right moment, being only extraordinary in showing greater sensitivity than his contemporaries. For many already were beginning to see the same visions. Hume said of him: 'He has only felt during the whole course of his life. He is like a man who was stripped, not only of his clothes, but of his skin.' He therefore felt the slings and arrows more keenly than his fellows, even when he had provoked them himself; but he felt too the peace of high places which has consoled many after him. He emphasized and put into words what others were coming to see, and he developed in them the attitude of mind which would climb what he himself did not dare. His is a strange fate. It is curious that Rousseau the timid should have been hailed by the Revolution as its herald. It is equally remarkable that Hitler and the totalitarian state should be considered by some as rooted in his doctrine. Bertrand Russell has claimed that 'the dictatorships of Russia and Germany, but particularly the latter, are in part the outcome of Rousseau's teaching'. Hence the thought, stranger still, that even before Nietzsche he may have given birth to the nationalistic German climber of the twentieth century, armed with iron pitons which are to take him with infinite toil and danger up the most inaccessible rock face. Here is the 'reductio ad absurdum' of a religious devotion. Here is our devotee to whom the mountains are all in all, who is not happy unless he is buffeted by the elements, a part with his mother Nature in her fiercest mood and yet fighting her too for his own or his country's glory. He is Rousseau's heir. He too, the psychologists would tell us, is yearning back to a mother; he attempts an escape through her which is both a 'rêverie'—for he is necessarily a dreamer—and a realization of what he imagines to be himself. Rousseau would be surprised indeed, more surprised than we at first imagined, to find for what progeny he has been responsible.

De Saussure, Pioneer of Science

Les hautes aiguilles, vues de profil, se subdivisent en une forêt de pyramides qui ferment l'enceinte de ce cirque et qui semblent destinées à défendre l'entrée de cette charmante retraite et à y conserver l'innocence et la paix.

HORACE BÉNÉDICT DE SAUSSURE is the best-known of the scientific Alpinists. No second ascent in history has achieved the fame of his climb on Mont Blanc in 1787, nor have biographers been so attracted either by the feats or the personality of any other pioneering scientist. This essay therefore must avoid trespassing from its short compass over ground too well covered before. It must keep strictly as its purpose the correct placing of de Saussure among the literary personalities we have assembled, and an assessment of his influence on the course of mountaineering. This assessment can best be made if we look in turn at his philosophy of life, the extent of his scientific achievement and the literary and human quality of his work. There is no room to stray into the fields of scientific detail or of political experiences. If he is to be the father of scientific Alpinism, his claim to the title must rest on an estimate of these three facets of his personality.

The first of course implies the other two. De Saussure could not have made novel scientific discoveries if he had not held a certain view of his own place and that of science in life. He was fortunate in his forerunners and in his environment. He stands heir to the Swiss, Conrad Gesner, the bold Renaissance figure who as early as the sixteenth century could almost from his adventures be styled father of the Alpine Clubs. In his own time he owed most to Albrecht von Haller, a Genevese botanist for whom he was collecting plants on his first journey to Mont Blanc in 1760. Such men and the atmosphere of eighteenth-century Geneva bred in him an outlook on the hills primarily scientific. The object of his first *Voyage* is indicative. He himself, in the 'Discours Préliminaire' to the *Voyages dans les Alpes* states the purpose of his life work. His study is the study of the Earth. 'It is above all through the study of mountains that the progress of a theory of the Earth can be accelerated.' This claim must be kept in mind always. He was first a scientist, then a traveller. For it was 'not enough to follow the high roads' in order to be admitted into the 'workshop of Nature'. The true scientist must undergo what were then great hardships if he was to make his valuable experiments between sea level and 16,000 feet. Thus of the very summit of Mont Blanc, which came to him almost as an anticlimax, he writes: 'My object was not only to reach the highest point, I was bound to make the scientific observations and experiments which alone gave value to my venture.' He meant what he said, though it seems a hard saying. Four and a half hours he spent in activity with hygrometer, electrometer, and thermometer, hours 'limited by the difficulty in my breathing', and even so he expressed regret 'at not having got all I hoped out of it'. It was science then that first set his foot upon the slopes.

With the scientific attitude followed naturally a deep interest in the men who inhabit high valleys. The peasants spring alive from his pages, because he knew all about them, about their methods of making hay or of passing winter evenings. He was interested objectively in their characters, in personalities like the young woman whom he met walking her lover to his home, in order to find out whether he had enough to support her. The Chamoniards he came to know intimately from his first visit in 1760, and to be so respected by them that they would take off their hats in the street at his name. He studied their system of agriculture and suggested a form of poor law. He described their habits, and even passions, in such language that the original French must be read. Take the chamois hunter. After the first failure, 'It is there that the huntsman's labours really begin. For then, carried away by his passion, he ceases to recognize danger. He crosses the snows, without a thought for the chasms which they may conceal. He undertakes the most dangerous routes, climbs, leaps from rock to rock without knowing how he will get down.'[17] There is real literature, as well as power of observation, in the account of the wife's anxieties at home, or in the story of the young man who prophesied his own certain death when he took up the chase. His prophecy was too true. Finally he sums up the attractions of the sport in words which link the cool scientist with the rashest of twentieth-century rock climbers:

But it is these very dangers, this alternation of hope and fear, the continual agitation kept alive by these sensations in his heart, which excite the huntsman, just as they animate the gambler, the warrior, the sailor, and even to a certain point the naturalist among the Alps,

[17] The original French is too picturesque to be omitted: C'est là que commencent les fatigues du chasseur. Car alors, emporté par sa passion, il ne connaît plus de danger; il passe sur les neiges, sans se soucier des abîmes qu'elles peuvent cacher; il s'engage dans les routes les plus périlleuses, monte, s'élance de rocher en rocher, sans savoir comment il en pourra revenir (*Premier Voyage*).

whose life resembles closely, in some respects, that of the chamois hunter.[18]

Finally and because of his deeper understanding of them he discovered in the peasants a wealth of good which Ruskin never appreciated. 'Those who see the peasant only in the environs of cities have no idea of the child of nature.' That is what we suspect, with Ruskin. To de Saussure they are friends.

The scientist approaches mountains and their place in religion with a free and open mind. It is difficult to find clues to the connection in de Saussure's thought between hills and worship, but one point is very certain. He would have none of the false superstition which had hitherto clothed the valleys. He spoke against it with a decisiveness remarkable only a century after the legends believed by the Jesuit Kirchner. Yet he was tolerant. A good Protestant, he paid handsome tribute to the monks of the St Bernard Hospice, and was a friend of the Abbé Murith who first climbed the Velan (12,358 feet). But he was terrified of the Roman Catholic clergy 'en masse': 'Next day I resumed my march, in spite of the urgent entreaties of M. l'Abbé, who wanted to take me to dine with the Curé of Notre Dame de la Gorge, where all the Curés of the neighbourhood were dining. I was so terrified at the idea of this fête that I went out of my way so as not to pass Notre Dame.' At the same time he would speak with some amusement of Madame Charlet, 'the lady who thought it such a pity I must be damned', or of the fears which haunted the inhabitants of the Vale of Chamonix. For by these the name of 'montagnes maudites' had been given to the chain of Mont Blanc in memory of crimes supposedly committed among

[18] Mais ce sont ces dangers mêmes, cette alternative d'espérance et de crainte, l'agitation continuelle que ces mouvements entretiennent dans l'âme, qui excitent le chasseur, comme elles animent le joueur, le guerrier, le navigateur, et même jusqu'à un certain point le naturaliste des Alpes, dont la vie ressemble bien à quelques égards à celle du chasseur des chamois (*Premier Voyage*).

the snows. 'This superstitious idea, quite absurd though it is, has certainly been able to serve as foundation for an unfavourable impression.' Or he is amused at a certain credulous bailiff's theory about the age of the world. The most that can be said of de Saussure's own view is that, while a Protestant, he had already worked towards a theory of the Evolution of the Universe; and that one thing which his scientific studies had taught him was the microscopic insignificance of man in comparison even with the mountains of his own earth. It is man's duty therefore to be tolerant of the views of others when they are sincerely held. Soon after his stay in Rome, where his small daughter Albertine had been kissed by the Pope, the family visited Voltaire. 'If she has been kissed by the Pope, then she must be kissed by the anti-Pope too,' Voltaire said. And Albertine accepted the kiss. To such a philosophy, excessive ambition is as absurd as fanaticism. 'When from the summit of Etna he sees under his feet two Empires that in other times nourished millions of warriors, how puerile must ambition appear to him!'

Finally, for all his scientific coolness, de Saussure nourished an unreasoning passion for high places which he could neither conceal nor explain either to himself or to his wife. He married in 1765 at the age of twenty-five and before the majority of his extensive journeys in the Alps. His attempts at persuading his wife and allaying her fears are amusing evidence of the distraction of his affections. A certain passage in one of his letters is well known:

In this valley, which I have not previously visited, I have made observations of the greatest importance, surpassing my highest hopes; but that is not what you care about. You would rather—God forgive me for saying so—see me growing fat like a friar and snoring every day in the chimney corner after a big dinner than that I should achieve immortal fame by the most sublime discoveries, at the cost of reducing my weight by a few ounces and spending a few weeks away from you.

Few mountaineering husbands have as good excuse as de Saussure. At other times he will genuinely try to spare her by not telling the worst until after, and then telling it with humour. His Monte Rosa tour he made after he had already promised 'No more'. He therefore felt an especial guilt when he wrote of the Pizzo Bianco under Monte Rosa itself:

I said nothing to you about this mountain, although the wish to visit it was the chief motive of my journey, because I was afraid you would imagine that I wanted to reach the highest peak, which is still virgin and will, I expect, remain so eternally, like your friend Mademoiselle M.

It was small wonder that Madame de Saussure wished to keep her husband under her eye, even if that eye must be telescopic, when he made his ascent of Mont Blanc. Yet the couple remained devoted. Perhaps she realized that this was a passion no less overwhelming because it was inexplicable by a devotion to science. It was a necessary impulse which did nothing to diminish his affection for her. She may have seen, like his uncle M. Bonnet, that he 'had two wives, or rather two mistresses, the mountains and his wife'. He came back to her each time. On the dizzy heights, as they seemed, of the Col du Géant he wrote with a deep love: 'Neighbour of Heaven though I am, I am very far from being detached from earthly objects.'

De Saussure's scientific work must be judged with an eye on Roussy's description of him as 'créateur de l'alpinisme scientifique'. We have seen that he approached in the spirit strictly of scientific inquiry, even if his approach concealed a greater passion than he realized for the heights themselves. We must consider here, not the extent of his knowledge, but how far his approach was novel, how far he was the source of a feeling towards mountains which he transmitted to the nineteenth-century scientific explorers. It is hard, to begin with, to realize upon what a fresh field he started. There is no space for detail; but the work of the credulous Scheuchzer in the previous century, of Grüner and of Altmann were either unknown or had to be ignored by him. He confessed that in 1760 he was not familiar with Grüner's work. In the case of glaciers, for instance, some of the beliefs held about the causes of their existence and motion were wild to the point of superstition. Great then was the importance of de Saussure's 'Théorie du mouvement des glaciers sous l'action de leur poids'. Even the terms 'glacier' (previously 'glacière'), 'moraine' and 'sérac' were introduced by him into scientific literature; others, such as 'roches moutonnées', were of his own invention. He made many mistakes, inevitably, as in his theory of medial moraines. That is not important. It is the scientific approach as set out in his 'Discours Préliminaire' which is both impressive and important, the willingness to experiment and to reject views which are shown to be untenable. For the sake of such experiments he was prepared to go to great lengths. In 1787, after the ascent of Mont Blanc, he camped with his son at a height of 10,959 feet on the Col du Géant in order to complete what he had not been able to do on the summit of the mountain. During their stay de Saussure himself would go to bed at midnight and rise at seven, his son would rise at four to continue the experiments. They were driven down after a fortnight by the guides, who destroyed their provisions. But their readiness to bear fatigue and what was then considered 'privation' in the cause of science marked the foundation of the new school. (This privation was by later standards not very severe. On Mont Blanc there had been eighteen guides, carrying, among other items, 'a bed, mattresses, sheets, coverlets and a green curtain'. Clothes included 'two green greatcoats, two night-shirts and three pairs of shoes'.) It matters little that de Saussure reckoned the Matterhorn the third-highest summit in the Alps, and failed to notice the Weisshorn and Dom. It matters no more that the actual mountaineering technique then employed was so unscientific that guides very often did not think of putting on the rope over glaciers and were sometimes saved by a miracle from disaster. These were early days. It was at this very time that Rousseau was peddling theories about the 'snowy heights', for which he showed a conspicuous dislike when it came to treading them himself. De Saussure was at the least an adequate performer on rocks, for it is impossible to believe the extravagances of Bourrit. He was besides interested as a scientist in the young craft of ice and snow. 'We arm our feet with ice-claws [crampons] which assure our foothold and allow us to accelerate our pace.' Or he gives an accurate account of the glissade, 'upright on the feet, body leaning backward and supported by an iron-shod stick'. Here too then writes the father of the new Alpinism.

It remains to consider the literary and 'general' quality of his writing. The British scientist J. D. Forbes said of him: 'There is scarcely one of our more modern writers with whom I am acquainted whose writings can be compared with those of de Saussure.' This is a judgement upon his literary as well as his scientific merit. Some of that breadth and charm which make the literary worth of the *Voyages* can be seen already from the passages quoted. There is crispness and accuracy in the description, humour and a human understanding pressed between the pages to make the whole absorbing to the least scientific of readers. For it is that breadth of de Saussure's interest which first awakens curiosity, as it is his humanity which fascinates thereafter. He was nothing if he was not humane and generous. At the age of twenty he could offer, on his first visit to Chamonix, a reward to the first man up Mont Blanc. Later he could see Dr Paccard and Jacques Balmat before him to the top, and be possessed only of a generous enthusiasm to follow their steps, while he speaks in glowing terms of their courage and resolution. There is but one passage which shows him human enough to be faintly jealous. He writes of Paccard: 'He seems to have taken pains everywhere to have gone a little further and a little

The Ascent to the Col du Géant

higher than I have been.' But he would have been too good
to be true had he not written so. Yet more surprising, he
was able to tolerate the flamboyant Bourrit, who first
persuaded him to their joint attack by the Aiguille de
Goûter in 1785 and then made utterly false and provoca-
tive accusations. 'I could not but notice that the way you
came down was not the happiest. . . .' De Saussure's
magnanimity in answering his charges was beyond praise.
He had already made clear that he preferred to go alone:
'I always prefer to make ascents of this nature alone with
my guides. But M. Bourrit . . .' Now, however, he utters
scarcely a direct reproach, but replies in the most generous
terms. He even, in the *Voyages*, refers to Bourrit as a good
Alpinist (which he certainly was not), while he sensibly
determines to have none of his company on the climb in
1787, and will take no share in the jealous attempt to
blacken Paccard's character. The truth was that their two
temperaments were utterly different: Bourrit impetuous,
poetic, unstable; de Saussure the scientist, rational and at
the same time generous because he saw the absurdity of
being otherwise. Of the two, it is the latter we admire
and love.

It was not only his quality as a warm-hearted observer
of men that made de Saussure's writing literature. There
is extremely little scenic description, for he seldom allowed
himself anything not germane to his purpose. But out of
the very purposefulness of his style a tool has been forged
which has given polish and distinction to the descriptive
passages of the *Voyages* such as he would never have
claimed. He wrote of himself that he was 'more accustomed
to climb rocks than to turn polished phrases'. Yet he could
describe and appreciate the beauty of Monte Rosa above
the Val d'Anzasca. To Ruskin it was to be 'A white heap
with no more form to it than a haycock after a thunder
shower'. Nor would anyone wish to deny the title of literature to his description of the view over the forest of

E

Aiguilles seen from the hut under the Aiguille du Goûter. Characteristically, after what he might have thought a purple passage, he goes on to recount the setting up of thermometer and hygrometer. More poetic is a description of sunset and nightfall over Mont Blanc. When the sun is gone he comes out, alone:

> The sky was then perfectly pure and cloudless, and the vapour could be seen no more except at the bottom of the valleys. The stars were bright but shorn of any vestige of twinkle. They shed over the mountain summits a very weak, pale light, but it was sufficient to distinguish masses and distances. The quiet and the deep silence which reigned over this vast expanse, magnified too by imagination, inspired in me a kind of terror. It was as if I were the last survivor of the Universe, and saw its corpse stretched under my feet.[19]

Douglas Freshfield, in a complete and sympathetic biography of de Saussure, adds his claim that his influence on the future of mountaineering was greater even than that of Rousseau; for Rousseau chipped no more out of the mountains than a peg on which to hang his theories about corrupt mankind. De Saussure's approach was more intelligent, if his readers were more limited. At least those readers were the enlightened of his day; the style of his writing has come down, through the best of the scientific pioneers, to the twentieth century, where the language of Himalayan travel has often the conciseness and blunt beauty of some passages of the *Voyages*. It is the merit of these writers that they can describe objectively and never be dull; the story is too absorbing. It is their merit too that

[19] The French is not to be translated, and it should be read as French:

Le ciel était alors parfaitement pur et sans nuages, la vapeur ne se voyait plus que dans le fond des vallées; les étoiles brillantes, mais dépouillées de toute espèce de scintillation, répandaient sur les sommités des montagnes une lueur extrêmement faible et pâle, mais qui suffisait pourtant à faire distinguer les masses et les distances. Le repos et le profond silence qui régnaient dans cette vaste étendue, aggrandie encore par l'imagination, m'inspiraient une sorte de terreur; il me semblait que j'avais survécu seul à l'univers, et que je voyais son cadavre étendu sous mes pieds.

whatever the story, it can be relied upon for accuracy and for truth, for a moderation and justice which de Saussure carried over himself into the stormy Revolution politics of Geneva. Possibly this sense of balance denied to him that 'spirit of rashness' which makes the pioneer of first ascents. He was not primarily interested in such. Bourrit's attempts inspired his ascent of Mont Blanc, it was the advice of Exchaquet which set him on the Col du Géant. He is not the less lovable for that, nor is his example the less to be followed by us who count our peaks, who have no ear for natural lore because we must be scampering without stop to the highest or hardest summit. It would be well with us, could we also temper our love of feats with a desire for unclouded knowledge. Yet there is a ring of despair in de Saussure's own words: 'Placed on this planet since yesterday, and only for one day, we can but desire knowledge to which, seemingly, we shall never attain.'

Goethe, the Romantic Man

Der Einsamkeiten tiefste schauend unter meinem Fuss
Betret' ich wohlbedächtig dieser Gipfel Saum.

WE expect Goethe to be a mountaineer. He who was looked upon by his own age as representative of every interest and faculty, the scholar, poet, statesman, artist, scientist whom Napoleon himself respected—he must surely have found a place on his wide horizon for these important items of Nature's equipment.

Next, we should expect him to have gone through two phases in his feeling for hills, as he did in his outlook on everything else. First the period of 'Storm and Stress', when the 'Wanderer' flung himself upon his adored:

> *Fresh nurture and new strength of blood*
>   *From the free world suck I.*
> *Nature to me is fair and good.*
>   *Who on her bosom lie.*
>
> *Our boat is cradled by the wave*
>   *In time with the oar's beat*

[69]

The mountains cloud-capped, heaven-high,
Watch us, and hail and meet.[20]

We should expect too that he would associate the mountains with the various women he loved even more passionately and certainly than did Petrarch, and that storm or sun upon the heights would sound the refrain to his own selfish emotions. Then in later years we should look for a more tranquil state, for an interest dispassionate as it was scientific, in short for the 'classic' repose. What we above all expect from 'the most versatile man of his century' is a many-sidedness of attitude towards the many sides of mountain experience.

These expectations are in the main realized. The young Goethe had begun as a dandy in the rococo school at Leipzig. But in 1770 he went at the age of nineteen to Strasburg, where he was to be affected deeply by the twin experiences of his meeting with Herder and his love for Friederike Brion. He came to take that passionate view of Nature in her relation to man which was later the foundation stone of the 'Sturm und Drang' movement. Yet it is not surprising to find even in the emotional young man a determined, even a 'cold', approach to some aspects of his relation with her. Her lover, yes, but he liked to be the master too. Now there were some natural sensations which made him uncomfortable, indeed which he could not tolerate without physical disgust. He was nervously susceptible to loud noises and he could not look down from a height without a sick feeling of giddiness. Of the former affliction he cured himself at Strasburg by walking each evening near the drums

[20] Und frische Nahrung, neues Blut
Saug' ich aus freier Welt.
Wie ist Natur so hold und gut,
Die mich am Busen hält!

Die Welle wieget unser Kahn
Im Rudertakt hinauf,
Und Berge wolkig himmelan
Begegnen unserm Lauf.

when they were beating their loudest. In the case of the giddiness, he describes his method in *Dichtung und Wahrheit* as follows, and it is one whose principle has been the saving of many nervous mountaineers since Goethe's day:

I would climb alone to the top of the cathedral tower, where I sat in the 'neck', under the 'bulb' or 'crown', as it is variously named. I remained perhaps a quarter of an hour before I dared to step out on to a slab, scarcely a yard square, from which, without any special support, one looks straight over the endless countryside, while the near surroundings, the cathedral ornaments and everything upon which one is standing are hidden. It is exactly as if one were raised in a balloon up through the air. This painfully frightening experience I repeated until it was quite indifferent to me. I have since drawn great benefit from these exercises, both on mountain journeys, in my geological studies and in large buildings, where I have been able to compete with the carpenters in treading unfenced balconies and cornices fearlessly. . . .

Very different is his approach from that of Rousseau, dizzily peeping over the parapet and enjoying the giddy sensations that beset his head.

For it is the scientist already speaking here, a scientist who persisted in shadowing even the young, passionate Goethe of 'Sturm und Drang'. To this amorous Goethe the Nature of mountains and lakes became firmly harnessed to his various loves, to Friederike Brion, to Charlotte Buff or Lili Schönemann. Like his own Werther he came to regard the two elements of his being as so closely bound that the scenery could no longer be enjoyed for itself alone. Looking over the peaks from the St Gotthard Pass he was constrained to exclaim:

Lili my darling, if I loved you not,
Then oh what joy this view had given me![21]

For to Switzerland he had gone, in 1775, at the suggestion of the two young and admiring Stolbergs. The decision to make the journey had been taken suddenly, in the middle of, and almost as a relief from, his affair with Lili. At Zürich he was glad to exchange the lively pair for the more

[21] Wenn ich, liebe Lili, dich nicht liebte,
  Welche Wonne gäb' mir dieser Blick!

placid Passavant, with whom he made his first ascent of the St Gotthard. The travellers were surprised that the pious father at the hospice could find enjoyment in living alone among such savage surroundings. At the top of the pass itself Goethe sat and sketched the hills. His companion suggested a descent to the valleys of Italy stretched before them. But Goethe could not decide to follow. 'Wenn ich, liebe Lili, dich nicht liebte. . . .' He stood up suddenly, to put aside such temptation:

I then turned to the path by which we had ascended. My friend followed me with some hesitation, and despite his loving dependence on me he remained for some time at a certain distance behind, until the splendid waterfall brought and held us together again. . . .

Of the descent I will say no more than that we found the snow-bridge over which we had walked some days before with a heavily laden parry quite collapsed. We were compelled to a detour to cross the yawning gulf and admired the vast ruins of Nature's architecture.

He was still at this stage young enough almost to be touched by the romance of earlier superstition. 'Here it would need but little imagination to fancy dragons' nests in the crevices.' Certainly he was young and lively enough still for play, for frolicsome bathing-parties and stone-throwing with the Stolbergs.

His next important journey was that undertaken to the Harz mountains in the winter of 1777. Goethe had by this time entered the service of the Duke of Weimar, Karl August. On this occasion it is the pretext of the journey which is 'scientific'; its real cause and the outcome are poetic. For the Duke had proposed a boar hunt to clear the forests of Eisenach. It was decided that Goethe should make a detour through the Harz, visit a young man, whose melancholy from reading overmuch *Werther* needed cheering, and inspect the Duke's copper mines. The real reason, however, unconfessed, is the poetic desire to make a winter ascent of the Brocken, the highest mountain in the Harz. This he tells to Charlotte von Stein in a letter:

I will reveal to you (don't tell anyone) that my journey to the Harz was made because I wished to ascend the Brocken; and now, my

Faustus and Mephistopheles before the Brocken

Engraved by Henry Moses

dearest, I have been up there today, quite all right, although everybody has been assuring me for the last eight days that it was impossible. . . . I have a longing for the full moon. And now, my dearest, I go
out of the door and there lies the Brocken in the sublime, splendid
moonlight above the pine trees. Today I was up there, and I offered the
most heartfelt thanks to God upon the witches' altar.

The poem which he wrote, 'Harzreise im Winter', is no
description, except in a sentimental sense, of a journey
which for those days was severe enough. He set out on
November 20th determined to climb the mountain in spite
of bad weather and two feet of snow. He climbed it early
in December, and wrote in his diary: 'Snow three feet
deep, but bearing. On top at 1.15 p.m. Cheerful, splendid
moment, the whole world wrapt in cloud and mist, but all
clear above. "What is man that thou art mindful of him?"
Back at 4.0.' In his own notes to the poem he gives a more
elaborate description of the view, but he still hardly indi-
cates his true theme. For the mountain, the Brocken, is a
mountain still associated with the beloved, but by now in a
calmer spirit of gratitude. The personal importance of individual man has become very much smaller. The 'Harzreise'
is a paean of thanksgiving, to Charlotte for her goodness
and to the Duke for his reception of the poet at friendly
Weimar. The 'Father of Love' is therefore invoked. There
is an outpouring of gratitude for the path which it is given
him by this power to tread over ground that might else
have been rough and lonely, but is now safely moonlit. The
warmth of love can make the elements themselves laugh.

> *So with the myriad colours of morning*
> *You laugh to his heart;*
> *So with the stinging of storm*
> *High you bear him aloft.*
> *Winter streams from the rocks come plunging*
> *To sing his psalms.*
> *Altar now of his thankfulness*
> *Is the dread summit's*
> *Snowy hung crown,*

Which with the ghost legions
Once the believers peopled.[22]

The mountains are still with him then, but illumined more quietly by a thankfulness for the narrow way allowed among them. It is no longer demanded that they figure as the sympathetic background to his dark passions.

The next visit to Switzerland therefore is more sedate. The period of 'Storm and Stress' did not end on the day in 1775 when he entered the Court of Weimar. But by 1779 he was looking with a more dispassionate eye at the hills around; dispassionate and yet interested, since he is better prepared now to examine mountains in their rôle as large objects worthy of his scientific curiosity. On this journey he had visited both Friederike and Lili; he had left them, it is true, but he recalled their loves with pleasure and without regret. For he had a strange capacity for digesting experiences, creditable or discreditable. Now he passed on through the mountain ravines. The description of one of these in *Dichtung und Wahrheit* is so significant that it must be quoted, though it was scarcely mountaineering and though the prose is turgid and redundant.

The journey through the narrow pass gave me a great, calm feeling. . . . My eye and my soul could encompass the objects, and since I myself was pure and the feeling could never offend or become false, the things about me made a proper and legitimate impression. If we compare such feeling with that under which we laboriously struggle with petty things and energetically strive to imbue these petty things with all that can possibly be imparted to them, and embellish them according to our ability in order to give our mind enjoyment and batten it on its

[22] Mit dem tausendfärbigen Morgen
    Lachst du ins Herz ihm;
    Mit dem beizenden Sturm
    Trägst du ihn hoch empor;
    Winterströme stürzen vom Felsen
    In seine Psalmen,
    Und Altar des lieblichen Danks
    Wird ihm des gefürchteten Gipfels
    Schneebehangner Scheitel,
    Den mit Geisterreihen
    Kränzten ahnende Völker.

own creation, then we see for the first time that we are concerning ourselves with a paltry makeshift.

Of this passage Georg Brandes wrote:

Goethe has consciously taken leave of the sentimental view of
Nature from his early days, the view that he ascribes to Werther when
he has him find Nature now effusively good, now merely destructive,
entirely dependent on his own joyful or depressed mood. Goethe has
now, in peaceful contemplation, transformed the soul into a mirror, a
pure mirror of and for Nature that stands out unassailable by the
changing moods of mortal man.

The descriptions then are factual and few human beings
appear, as if they were 'too small to be of interest in this
exalted natural scenery'. He is concerned now with a
'larger life'. 'One dimly guesses at the origin and life of
these strange shapes. However and whenever such things
came to be, these masses have fused into large, simple
forms. . . .' A meeting with de Saussure at Geneva stimulated in him a further interest in the physical sciences
among mountains. But as for the human creature amid
such grandeur—he is out of place. The lofty scientist and
philosopher could now no more be caught climbing a hill
'for its own sake' than he would countenance the Duke's
over-boisterous notions about rolling stones 'à la Rousseau'
down the glacier. The Duke loved dearly to trundle. But
what little sense of humour Goethe may have had now
abandoned him, and he wrote: 'I told him that would do
and we couldn't get any more fun out of it.' The remark
has almost the solemnity of 'we are not amused'. But fortunately besides his prose he was writing poetry. Waterfalls had impressed him always, perhaps more than snows.
On October 9th they visited the Staubbach falls near
Lauterbrunnen in the Bernese Oberland. The poem which
he wrote after this visit, 'Gesang der Geister über den
Wassern', is 'the submissive mood of "Grenzen der
Menschheit" developed almost to complete subjection. . . .
Man is now subject to cosmic laws, fulfilling his destiny
according to these laws. . . . The strength and "Sturm und

Drang" vitality have disappeared. No emphasis is laid on human volition. . . .' It is none the less a magnificent poem, a sublimation of the experience of watching mountain water falling, until it comes to represent the human soul descending from heaven and returning to it:

> *The soul of man*
> *Is water too,*
> *Comes from the sky,*
> *To sky returns,*
> *Then down to earth*
> *Must fall once more;*
> *Eternal change.*
>
> *So from the high*
> *Steep rocky wall*
> *The clear stream shoots. . . .*[23]

There is this perpetual surprise for the student of Goethe: however dispassionate he appears, however rigidly the classic mask tightens over his features, the poetic self in him is invincible and streams out just when we were expecting his views on mineralogy or comparative religion. The very next year he wrote what has been described as the most perfect mountain poem ever written, for ever quoted and never stale:

> *Over all the hilltops*
> *Is rest,*
> *In all the treetops*
> *You may sense*
> *Hardly a stir.*

[23] Des Menschen Seele
Gleicht dem Wasser:
Vom Himmel kommt es,
Zum Himmel steigt es
Und wieder nieder
Zur Erde muss es,
Ewig wechselnd.

Strömt von der hohen
Steilen Felswand
Der reine Strahl. . .

The birds are quiet in the wood.
Only wait, soon now
You will rest, too.[24]

The poem was written on the evening of September 6th
on the wall of a shooting-box on the Gickelhahn, the
highest of the hills round Ilmenau. Its theme is peace,
peace among the mountains, and the English scientist John
Tyndall, an Alpinist too, remarked that its atmosphere was
so peaceful that he could almost see the thin lines of smoke
rising lazily from cottages. It is not strange then that in his
letter to Charlotte von Stein Goethe refers to the rising
smoke of the charcoal-burners' fires. The hilltops have been
touched with the quiet of acquiescence. This was an
acquiescence that had prevented him already from active
mountain-climbing for its own sake, indeed stifled the
mood for it. But it was not to quench scientific curiosity
nor prevent scientific exploits, since in his theory it was
given to man at least to 'know' and to be the 'mirror' of
that Nature. For Goethe, like some of our other personalities, inclined to interpret his mountains as he wished them
in order to fit his divine pattern. Thus at Ilmenau the out-
door life led him to geology. 'The mountains and ravines
promise me much entertainment. It is true that they do
not *now* strike me as so picturesque and poetic—but it is
merely a different sort of painting and poetry that they
suggest to me, when I go climbing among them.' The
italics are my own. For in that 'now' is seen the full portrait
of Goethe the calm classic, imagining himself no longer to
be moved spontaneously by the sight of a beautiful hill but
able to detach petty humanity from the background which

[24] Über allen Gipfeln
Ist Ruh,
In allen Wipfeln
Spürest du
Kaum einen Hauch;
Die Vöglein schweigen im Walde.
Warte nur, balde
Ruhest du auch.

earlier had seemed a living part of his own fibre. He still believed, certainly, that he had tasks left to do. Once on a steep slope he had to stand upon the shoulders of his forester-guide to break off an interesting fragment of red granite with blue-black tone on the surface. The guide complained of the danger, and Goethe cried: 'No matter, let's go on. We have both great things to do before we break our necks.' Emil Ludwig exclaims: 'He was President of an aristocratic Chamber, a poet of European reputation, a cold and misanthropic official—and from those lips broke those words, as he craned from the shoulders of a guide to touch the primeval rock. We might still be in Strasburg.' The truth of the matter may be that in this case Goethe's interest was not primarily in the 'great' things he was to do. He was excited out of himself by the rocks, 'the most steadfast, the most infrangible product of Nature. To me, who have suffered and still suffer from my fellow creatures' opinions, it may surely be granted to enjoy the sublime repose afforded by proximity, in solitude and silence, to the great heart of Nature which speaks to our hearts so gently.' He was not then reverting only to Strasburg enthusiasms when he risked his neck after red granite.

The last journey to Switzerland, in 1797, was the most prosaic. Conscientious descriptions of waterfalls, flowers, and rocks face us in short, unemotional sentences. The party climbs the Schwyzer Hacken, and an impression is given of the view: 'The mountain tops were all covered with manifold cloud and mist, so that their shapes could seldom be seen and for the most part only guessed. A strange light among the cloud and mist indicated sunset. These veils lay so thick one upon the other that at nightfall it was hardly credible that day would ever break again.' The old fire is lost. Goethe is settling down to the cold but interested calm of old age, and this was when he was but a year older than de Saussure after the ascent of Mont

Blanc. Even the sensation of quick and easy movement is ascribed not to the power of love but to the tonic quality of the air. 'We were back at the Hospice astonishingly soon, and ascribed our speed to the mountain air.' The rest of the journey loses itself in facts and figures.

He continued his scientific interest to the end, but had no more opportunity to practise on a large scale in mountain country. Probably he had not the wish. For like other experiences, like the love he bore to women, the mountain episode had served its turn, and he was ready to pass on to the next experience in line, to assimilate and to convert that too to literature. He was prepared now for the completion of *Faust* Part I, and to go on to the second *Faust*, redeemed by high philosophy and serving mankind by building dams. Rocks and hills remained, in the background of his scene, for they served a more abiding purpose than could Friederike Brion. They were constant reminders. But mountaineering, or the desire to climb heights for their own sake, had passed. In old age Goethe, talking with Eckermann, remarked that everybody passes a stage when he is Werther. He may have felt similarly that the 'complete' man is at one period of his life spiritually a mountaineer.

The Wordsworths

the storm, that drives
The traveller to shelter, summoned him
Up to the mountains.

1

I WAS tramping over the shoulder of Loughrigg above Grasmere on my way to the Youth Hostel where I hoped to spend the night. My sack was heavy and I suspected that the hostel would be full. It was stupid indeed to have come. I had chosen the worst of all seasons, Easter, to forsake the secluded cliffs of Cader Idris and the wild stony Rhinogs. I had come up by the night train, and although it was now hardly nine o'clock the tourist hordes were out already. I seemed to espy the ant cluster around what looked like Dove Cottage, the beetle line of buses on the road that winds down the pass from Keswick. It was very foolish to have come, I thought.

For I hardly dared to confess it to myself, I had come to pick up a long-cherished picture of Wordsworth as a mountaineer among his own mountains. Here is the father of our sport, I had said to myself, reading of the early attempts:

> *When I have hung*
> *About the raven's nest by knots of grass*
> *And half inch fissures in the slippery rock*
> *But ill sustained and almost, as it seemed,*

F

[81]

Suspended by the blast that blew amain,
Shouldering the naked crags, oh at that time
While on the perilous ridge I hung alone . . .

and again, his legs might look funny from behind, as even
Dorothy admitted, but he had covered more mountain
miles with them than any man of his day. Had he not been
the preacher of a faith in the beauty of mountains and their
villages almost wholly new in the eighteenth century,
only very faintly foreshadowed by the physically idle
Rousseau? I would come then and see what these hills of
his looked like; climb Silver Howe this afternoon, tomorrow make the long journey to Dow Crag and its cliffs
overlooking Coniston; the next day Eusemere, and so to
Helvellyn. I would see for myself.

Now the hills, I must admit, showed very much as I
had hoped, shapes as lovely as any poet could have wished.
But I had forgotten the valleys. At Rydal I had been over-
charged for breakfast. Grasmere Village as I entered it
looked like one large souvenir. The roads were thronged
with strapping, learned-looking Wordsworthians, each
with his competent pack and book, presumably of quotations. Dove Cottage as I now approached it was out of
the question. It was already full. I really could not, shabby
and unshaven, approach the austere dame who was telling
the assembled admirers the size of Dorothy Wordsworth's
oven and the number of guests that had assembled on the
18th of April 1802 . . . I must slink past.

A small boy was walking down the road, trailing his feet
in the dust. 'Where are you going?' he asked. I was going
to the Grasmere Youth Hostel. 'What are you?' I had
once been a climber. I showed him my boots. 'What are
those for? They look silly.'

He was small and brown and inquiring, sandy-haired
with freckles and a sunburn. 'I'm going to school,' he said.
'My school is over there, past the gingerbread shop. I'm
five and I'm in the second form now. You must go to the

gingerbread shop, you must get some Sarah Nelson's gingerbread.'

We had come down now from the high ground and our conversation seemed to have descended correspondingly to the fleshpots. I sighed and produced a toffee. It was accepted. 'Shall I eat it before school or in school or after school?' Each idea had attractive possibilities, to be debated at length. 'I think I'll eat it after school.'

We had passed the gingerbread shop now, and had arrived before 'Postcards—souvenirs of the Wordsworths'. I was in despair, the atmosphere was utterly wrong. Only my self-chosen guide remained, to trail his clouds of juvenile glory before me.

'What is your name?'

'Michael Wordsworth, and I'm the great-great-great-great- . . .'

I looked back at Loughrigg, which seemed to beam down suddenly. Perhaps then it might be well with me, after all. I seemed to have found what I had been looking for. I plumped the young Michael on a wall and photographed him, his ancestor's hills behind. Then we shook hands solemnly and parted. We might never meet again, but it had been enough. For me he had joined Wordsworth and his mountains, had put the picture into its final focus.

2

Petrarch had seen a divine significance in the prospect from a high mountain. Rousseau had longed to plunge himself into the 'bosom' of his mother Nature, to escape there the unfortunate persecutions of his own brothers. But he had never really shown interest in mountain formations for their own sake. It remained to study that Nature for herself and for the benign influence which she exerts upon those who inhabit her sanctuaries. This must now be done disinterestedly, without thought of her immediate effect on the student, except so far as it stimulates his poetic and generous imagination. The feeling for hills was growing gradually, we have seen, both in England and on the Continent throughout the eighteenth century. Richard Cumberland and others had sung the awesome sublimity of mountain scenery; Gray had shown a poetic sympathy with natural things. It remained still for a great poet and a great personality to fan the spark, to touch the whole with poetic fire until mountains[25] came to take their place as a necessary part of a complete philosophy.

William Wordsworth acknowledged his debt in matters of appreciation and companionship to his sister Dorothy, yet he never seemed to realize how much of his whole belief he owed her, how much she gave him when she came to keep him house and company at Dove Cottage by Grasmere. 'She pointed out to him that his office upon earth was to be a poet' (Leslie Stephen). Let us see her again for a moment, in the well-known description by De Quincey. 'Her face was of Egyptian brown'; her eyes were 'not soft, nor were they fierce or bold; but they were wild and startling, and hurried in their motion'. She was indeed like a wild thing, fashioned for the mountainside, not for the elegant parlour: for he goes on to remark upon 'the glancing quickness of her motions, and other circumstances in her deportment (such as her stooping attitude when walking) which gave an ungraceful, and even an unsexual character to her appearance when out of doors'. He did not see, it seems, that this character was that of the natural goer upon mountains. Her quickness, that readiness to walk, fitted her ideally to be the companion of her brother. In spirit too, we shall see, as in body she could lead and accompany him, could make pleasant his lonely heights and fill his barren places with hollows that were rich and green.

What new thing then did these two Wordsworths

[25] It was to be the mountains for themselves. Leslie Stephen wrote truly that 'he never cared . . . for history and tradition'.

come to seek together in the mountains? It was a measure of Dorothy's success with her brother that she helped to lead him away from the early restlessness and ignorance of a young man:

> *In youth from rock to rock I went,*
> *From hill to hill in discontent,*
> *Most pleased when most uneasy.*

She pointed him towards his later belief, whereby

> *Nature, intervenient till this time*
> *And secondary, now at length was sought*
> *For her own sake.*

That is to say he passed, with her as his comrade, through the phase of many of us who are mountain climbers. He began with his own sensations, enthusiasms, uneasiness; his own life seemed a conflict with his surroundings. Slowly, the mountains came to obtrude themselves as personalities by their own right, like that peak in the early *Prelude:*

> *a huge peak, black and huge*
> *As if with voluntary power instinct . . .*
> *Towered between me and the stars, and still,*
> *For so it seemed, with purpose of its own.*

These hills then became beings apart, moving, a modern poet has expressed it, 'between the Eternal Mode and mine'. Indeed they could be admonitory beings; it was the 'huge peak' that awoke a sense of guilt in him when he took the boat. They were at any rate half-personalities, set there by a benign Creator above us, but exerting influence for good on us:

> *huge and mighty forms, that do not live*
> *Like living men, moved slowly through my mind.*

In them was to be found an endless source of optimism, as at the end of the second book of the *Prelude* he tells. These higher phenomena of Nature go on and give hope, however distressed and weary our short human life may be. They have indeed power to transport us towards Heaven

[85]

itself, out of the gloom of human worry. Men have gone

Through the blind mist, I following, when a step,
A single step, that freed me from the skirts
Of the blind vapour, opened to my view
Glory beyond all glory ever seen. . . .

That glory was the view of distant mountains.

.   .   .   .   .

Let us ask then, looking through her *Journal*, just how far Dorothy Wordsworth prompted and shared the reverence for mountain and moor, this interest in them for their own sakes. She was, we have said, herself a walker, and enjoyed the physical sensation of movement among the hills. Indeed, De Quincey maintained, the later melancholy which clouded her life was due to 'an excess of pleasurable excitement and luxurious sensibility sustained in youth by a constitutional glow from animal causes but dropping as soon as that was withdrawn'. But then De Quincey was himself no great walker—or he might have seen that it was something more than animal which drove her to the fells. From the *Journal* we find that she walked, and would lead William to walk with her, simply because she loved passionately the ground she trod, and felt by walking in closer touch with it. 'I can always walk over the moors with a light foot; I seem to be drawn more closely to Nature in such places than anywhere else.' This was the answer. She was closer to 'Nature'; not only the simple Nature of valleys and trees and plants which to Rousseau seemed kind because men were not kind, but Nature in the widest sense, which gave to men themselves their kindness, as it provided the noblest principles by which they moved.

To go, then, into greater detail as to what these two together sought from their mountains: first, because they were interested in them, they studied their shapes as perhaps they had never been studied before. William's *Guide to the Lake District* is filled with advice as to the best view-

points. On the famous tour in Scotland in 1802 Dorothy
compared the forms of the Scottish hills not only with
those of the Lakes, but with themselves seen from different
viewpoints. Thus Ben Lomond from Luss 'did not seem to
me so large as Skiddaw does from Derwentwater' and
'there was something in the mountain that disappointed
me, a want of massiveness and simplicity, perhaps from
the top being broken into three distinct stages'. But as seen
from Glenfalloch 'the top of the mountain, being of a
pyramidal form, it is much grander than with the broken
outline, and stage above stage'. At other times there is
comparison between mountains seen through encircling
mist and those seen from top to base. The heights sur-
rounding Glencoe survived her test:

> It seldom happens that mountains in a very clear air look exceed-
> ingly high, but these though we could see the whole of them to their
> very summits, appeared to me more majestic in their own nakedness
> than our imaginations could have conceived them to be, had they
> been half hidden by clouds, yet showing some of their highest
> pinnacles.

Her quest then is for grandeur of form. She seeks next,
often enough, a simile that shall describe the effect of
grandeur produced upon herself. Very rarely she finds
herself at a loss; words fail her. 'Oh that I could describe,
nay that I could remember, the sublime spectacle of the
pinnacles and towers of Mont Blanc.' When she does discover it, this simile is not seldom a personification. Carefully selecting her viewpoint she says: 'Cruachan, on the
other side of the lake, was exceedingly grand, and appeared
of enormous height, spreading out two large arms that
made a cove down which fell many streams swollen by the
rain.' Or the Cobbler is 'a very craggy topped mountain
among other smooth ones, the rocks on the summit as
distinct in shape as if they were buildings raised up by
man, or uncouth images of some strange creature', and
again 'like a waggoner, his horse's head turned round
from us, the waggon behind with a covered top'. It is the

eye of childhood which sees in every mountain face a smile or a frown. It is the directness of childlike description which charms in Dorothy Wordsworth, which gave continually to William phrases which 'he could not get out of his head'.

As many have done since, Dorothy Wordsworth admired contrast in a mountain scene. She would not perhaps go so far as Dr Johnson, or maintain that any scene whatever is improved by the sight of a good inn in the foreground. But it is true, she says, that the harmony of height and habitation charms. On one occasion 'the encircling hills were so exquisitely formed that it was impossible to conceive anything more lovely than this place would have been, if the valley and hillsides had been interspersed with trees, cottages, green fields and hedgerows. But all was desolate.' Or it is the contrast between winter on the Jungfrau and the sunny fields and chalets of Wengernalp that is pleasing. For the idea of contrast, between hill and house, movement and rest, became fundamental to the Wordsworthian idea of mountains. It is the moving traveller reflected in the still lake (in the *Guide Book*) who focuses the eye; or the 'stationary blast of waterfalls', with its opposing principles of tranquillity and powerful motion, lures the two many miles out of their course to admire these, the microcosms of their Nature.

A little has been said already of the pleasure which the Wordsworths found in physical exertion. Theirs was indeed not movement purely for 'exercise', at any rate in the more mature years. William would not have been found on a rowing machine; nor probably would he have seen any point in climbing rocks for the sake only of climbing them and no more. He certainly found himself rock climbing, in quest of birds' nests for instance, as he shows in the famous description of his perilous climb for the raven's nest. But then it was the nest, or the 'loud dry wind' that had interested him, not primarily the per-

Grasmere seen from Loughrigg

formance of his own body. Or he climbed a boulder in
order to measure it: 'William climbed up the rock, which
would have been no easy task but to a mountaineer, and
we measured its height.' Yet however purely they enjoyed,
in the first place, the beauty of the hill they climbed, they
could not but in passing appreciate the pleasure of their
own sensations as they exerted themselves, whether pro-
ceeding from 'animal' or other causes. William was happy
indeed, skating on Windermere, to feel

> *Proud and exulting like an untired horse*
> *That cares not for his home.*

For they hated human things that were ugly, like the
landlady at Luss with her fat dropsical legs suspended in a
basin of hot water. They loved beauty of movement in
whatever form, their own or that of lithe boys or the
Highland girl, charming in her simplicity:

> *Thou wearst upon thy forehead dear*
> *The freedom of a mountaineer.*

Such a mountaineer was Dorothy Wordsworth herself,
with her stoop and her 'unsexual' gait. A mountaineer in
our sense was William, even if he needed to be guided over
the roof of Milan Cathedral by a hand 'steadier than his
own'; even if the legs which, De Quincey says, had carried
him many thousands of miles over the hills, appeared from
the back at times ridiculous. 'Miss Wordsworth would
exclaim, in a tone of vexation, "Is it possible? Can that be
William? How very mean he looks!" ' Had she but known
it, that very meanness of appearance, the stoop of the
shoulders and the sunken chest, spelt a better goer over
rough ground than Mr J. who walked beside him, 'a fine,
towering figure, six feet high, massy and columnar in his
proportions'.

Miss Wordsworth, then, realized as she walked that she
walked for pleasure. She enjoyed analysing that pleasure,
sipping the cup and comparing her method with that of
others. On Mount Saint Salvador 'none of the party rested

longer than was sufficient to recover breath. I did so frequently, for a few minutes; it being my plan at all times to climb up with my best speed for the sake of those rests, whereas Mary I believe never once sat down this morning, perseveringly mounting upward.' Or she compares herself with the poor woman toiling along the Highland road: 'I walked as she did, but pleasure was my object, and if toil came along with it even that was pleasure, at least it would be in the remembrance'. That being so, she did not necessarily feel compelled towards the windy tops, unless there were some special purpose in the visit. Her object was to enjoy and appreciate, not to conquer or mortify; just as her brother found the mountains gradually filling their own impregnable place, himself their disciple and companion. Therefore 'Attempted Fairfield, but misty' is a not uncommon type of entry: although even with the mist she succeeded in making friends. Thus another time 'as the mist thickened our enjoyment increased. At such times and in such places every scattered stone the size of one's head becomes a companion.' But, it must be confessed, this was on no more adventuresome path than the Kirkstone Pass; for on the whole, the Wordsworths found what they wanted below the 2,000-foot level, their vistas and their workshop on the gentle Loughrigg or White Moss, only rarely on the summits of Helvellyn or 'Scaw Fell'. Yet these higher tops too they insisted on visiting—unlike Southey or De Quincey—as a part of the mountain rite. They would have scorned a conveyance that could have brought them up without the exertion of the climb. On the Simplon Dorothy compares herself with a party moving by coach: 'I could not but congratulate myself on being on foot, for a hundred reasons the pleasantest mode of travelling in a mountainous country.' There is no doubt at all, whatever her ultimate object, she enjoyed using her limbs by the way, as does any mountain climber, for the pure pleasure of using them.

Finally the Wordsworths visited the mountains because of the persons whom they met there. Even so do we their modern visitors find in them our worthiest human contacts. They believed that the best men and women, the simplest and the most lovable, live among the hills. The 'Excursion' is in some sense a sermon on this theme. The 'Leech Gatherer', 'Michael' and a host of others are its examples. Many of these step first from Dorothy's *Journal*: the woman who asked 'What, are you stepping westward?'; the intrepid Swiss peasants who 'ascend with pikes and snow shoes, and on their return to the valley slide down, an appalling thought when the precipice was before our eyes and I almost shudder at the remembrance of it'; or the hospitable landlady by Loch Katrine. We too, whatever the 'Weltanschauung' whereby we view those mountains and whether we consider them beneficent personalities or indifferent lumps of rock and snow and grass, will continue to go to them for our happy companions, our kind hosts and our interesting acquaintances. In this debt, also, the Wordsworths were before us.

The comparison between the love of the Wordsworths for the hills and that of the Scotsman in the 'Excursion' is a little unfair. This imaginary person, to still the fever of love for beauty consuming him, compels himself to study objectively and in detail the scientific laws of light and colour on stormy waters, to plunge himself into scientific inquiry which he hopes will still the uneasy flames within. But in pursuing this course he finds the struggle too hard and his strength wastes away. So, it is said, did the Wordsworths, struggling through their own consuming passion for natural beauty in itself, find themselves old before their time. William at the age of thirty-nine was taken for sixty. Yet there is some truth in the comparison. They drove themselves hard, for it was 'exhausting' even to find the correct epithet for the cuckoo. It was perhaps in part the excitement of their hill discoveries, the constant companionship with adored Nature, that aged them prematurely, accounting for something of Dorothy's later melancholy and William's bad verse. It is not many who have tried to live intimately and on a high imaginative level with the hills over a long period. Moreover this was the first time that the experience had been seriously tried by a poet. Most of our outbursts are the better, perhaps, for being brief. We scuttle back, scared, into the society of the towns; we have not the chance either to tire ourselves or to sink into the unthinking routine of those who win their living from hill country. Yet how much do we miss, too, of the days when this experience was new and exciting; when the Kirkstone Pass was a venture and Scafell a major undertaking; when Dorothy could write pure poetry every time that she put pen to paper, be it on the most obvious theme. 'The stars in succession took their stations on the mountain tops', or 'At the end of a long valley we ascended a hill to a great height, and reached the top when the sun, on the point of setting, shed a soft yellow light upon every eminence.' De Quincey regretted that, for her own happiness of mind, this 'wild' woman had not read more widely, had not become a little more of the ordinary blue-stocking. But she would not, had she done so, have been Dorothy Wordsworth. She might have been a very capable wife to a very ordinary man instead of the astoundingly patient and inspiring sister to a poet whose temper must so often have been intolerable. She would not have enjoyed this new mountain joy upon which she lived and by describing which she pointed a way to the pioneers of the century that came after.

John Keats

I T has been said that the Romantic is he who interprets
Nature by himself. 'The romantic mind, stirred by a
view, begins to examine itself and the effect of the scenery
upon its emotions. The picturesque, on the contrary, turns
to the scene. . . .' Wordsworth, for all his study of hill
form, congratulated himself that he was immune from the
influence of these 'picturesque' travellers, the seekers after
comparison and the cataloguers of beauty spots:
for this,
Although a strong affection of the age,
Was never much my habit,—giving way
To a comparison of scene with scene,
Bent overmuch on superficial things.
In this sense he was a Romantic, as Shelley and Byron,
later, were Romantics. They, like him, were also teachers.
It is true that they were all three accurate observers as
well. A new note had been struck in poetry when Words-
worth wrote of his Leech Gatherer standing
As a huge stone is sometimes seen to lie
Couched on the bald top of some eminence

[93]

or Shelley described the glaciers

*Like snakes that watch their prey from their far fountains
   slow rolling on.*

Shelley and Byron liked besides to think of themselves as
Alpinists. Shelley wrote: 'I have been familiar from boyhood with mountains and lakes and the sea and the solitude
of forests; danger which sports upon the brink of precipices
has been my playmate; I have trodden the glaciers of the
Alps and lived under the eye of Mont Blanc.' It is difficult
to take his idea of danger on the cliffs too seriously. Byron
shows a liking for the picture of himself sitting upon some
mountain top, pouring scorn at ridiculous mankind below.
These two played, at any rate, at mountaineering. It was
part of the Romantic technique.

But however much they set out to be observers and men
of action, the suspicion creeps on us that what they were
really climbing was a mountain platform as decidedly, if
not quite so obviously, as Rousseau himself. Shelley likes
to preach his ideas at us, even if we think, with T. S. Eliot,
that they are 'ideas of adolescence', and that he often did not
know quite what he was preaching about. For him certainly
the mountains 'have "a voice to repeal large codes of fraud
and woe, not understood by all", and it is to be feared, not
very clearly understood by the poet himself'. The comment is
Leslie Stephen's. Even when his mountain description is at its
best, it is seldom allowed to pass without the didactic simile:

                                        The rushing snow,
The sun-awakened avalanche,—whose mass
Thrice sifted by the storm had gathered here,
Flake after flake, in heaven-defying minds
As thought by thought is piled, till some great truth
Is loosened, and the nations echo round,
Shaken to their roots, as do the mountains now.

Byron is either frankly 'popular':

        Mont Blanc is the monarch of mountains;
            They crowned him long ago
        On a throne of rocks, in a robe of clouds,
            With a diadem of snow—

[94]

or his pleasure is to sit like a godling on his imaginary
summit, reminding his fellows how small and ephemeral
they are in comparison with, for instance, a glacier:
> *Lo! Where it comes, like an eternity,*
> *As if to sweep down all things in its track.*

But, it must be repeated, the summits were largely
imaginary.

It is surprising to find John Keats stepping in among
these experienced Alpine travellers as a true Romantic.
He had never seen the Alps, still less had he dreamed of
inspiring acrobatic feats upon them. What would the
modern mountaineer, armed with rope and ice-axe, have
said of 'Mister John Keats, five feet high', who complained
of the wetness of a walk on the island of Mull, and whose
stomach was too delicate for a Scottish fare of eggs that
would have filled a Himalayan traveller with noble
delight? He would himself ask, then, how we had the
effrontery to set him here, away from the romantic galaxy.
Yet he has crept in somehow, we must try to assign him
his niche in the portrait gallery. And just because he did
not preach about them the impression of mountains may
be found, to our surprise, to have struck more deeply into
him than into the others; while at the same time he is
shown as a more competent performer than Byron with
his club-foot or Shelley who sat motionless when his boat
threatened to capsize.

Keats feigned to be lighthearted enough about it, certainly, to ward off the most earnest head-hunter. I am no
mountaineer at all, he would have said, a person put off
by the slightest difficulty. In June 1818 the famous tour
of Scotland began with a visit to Keswick and its falls,
and an ascent of Skiddaw. But the rocks, or rather the bogs,
by the falls of 'Lowdore' had him defeated. 'I had an easy
climb among the streams, about the fragments of rocks,
and should have got, I think, to the summit, but unfor-
tunately I was damped by slipping one leg into a squashy
hole.' And worse, the party had immediately before that

failed to ascend Helvellyn for mist. It was not at all venturesome, and the walk up to the Druids' stones, 'a fag uphill, rather too near dinner time', had tired him too, even if they made up for it next day by the now traditional ascent of Skiddaw, ten miles up and down before breakfast. Indeed to put off the scent those who would take him seriously as a mountain climber, Keats the sensualist has adopted quite deliberately the pose, light-hearted and serious too, of the experienced man who has seen through these things, to whom they are now no more than a commonplace. 'By this time', he later writes, 'I am comparatively a mountaineer. I have lived among wilds and mountains too much to break out much about their grandeur.' 'The first mountains I saw, though not so large as some I have since seen, weighed very solemnly upon me. The effect is wearing away, yet I like them mainly.' So it goes on. John Keats is determined that he shall not be mistaken for the real thing, for more than a person who has shown an intelligent interest and then passed on. A little of mountains, like a little oatcake, goes a long way.

For it is another dictum that the mountaineer, like the soldier, marches on his stomach, and to begin with our mountaineer John Keats was not the constitutionally strong person who could afford to play tricks with his body. His friends, who thought of him as robust, were surprised. 'But altogether', is the plaint in Scotland, 'this fare is too coarse. I feel it a little.' In these terms and stronger does he inveigh against the eternal Scottish oatcake. Or he complains of the eternal Scottish dampness, damp mist and misty hills: 'The road through the island [of Mull], or rather the track, is the most dreary you can think of, between dreary mountains, over bogs and rock and river with our breeches tucked up and our stockings in hand.' Or he is being fortified against the June cold on Skiddaw with a little rum, 'mixed, mind ye, with mountain water', two glasses going up and one returning. Or he is longing

[96]

John Keats

for his tea: 'I assure you, I often long for a seat and a cup
of tea at Well Walk, especially now that mountains, castles
and lakes are becoming common to me.' So the tale goes
on, and he can be imagined chuckling his glee at those who,
out of the bored aesthete, would elevate him suddenly to the
rank of active mountain pioneer.

Yet even on the score of physical exertion Keats cannot
altogether escape us. He was well built and physically
powerful. He climbed Skiddaw, as he said, without any
training, 'ten miles before breakfast' and felt none the
worse. He very soon had completed the 114 miles which
set him, with a further thirty-eight miles coach ride, inside
Scotland. He walked many leagues in Scotland. He and
Brown were prevented from completing their programme
partly owing to a sore throat—a sign of the approaching
consumption—but then they had lived harder throughout
than the Wordsworths, with whose journey their walk has
been sometimes compared. For the Wordsworths at times
rode or took a boat. Keats did his miles on foot. Besides,
they ascended Ben Nevis (Ah mio Ben!) and it 'is above
4,300 feet from the sea level'. It was 'almost like a fly
crawling up a wainscoat'. This climb he described in the
true spirit of the Victorian pioneers, with judicious ad-
mixture of hyperbole, the hyperbole we have noted in
Dante. 'The whole immense head of the Mountain is composed of large loose stones—thousands of acres.' 'We saw
still above us another huge crag, which still the Guide said
was not the top.' The Chasms are 'the most tremendous
places'—as indeed they are. The cold is sufficient even in
early August to make a glass of whisky very welcome 'now
and then'. Then the descent—for scree hopping in those
days was no more welcome than it is now. 'I have said
nothing yet of our getting on among the loose stones large
and small, sometimes on two, sometimes three, sometimes
four legs, sometimes two and stick . . . so that we kept on
ringing the changes on foot, hand, stick, jump, boggle,

G [97]

stumble, foot, hand, foot (very gingerly), stick again, and then again a game at all fours.' But to dissuade us from believing that this descent might in any sense be termed heroic ('May I be preserved from doing the like again', the pioneers would have said), there appears suddenly in the picture Mrs Cameron, '50 years of age and the fattest woman in Inverness-shire', who got up somehow—and down to tell the tale. But it remains a mystery how she did get down. As for Keats, 'I felt it horribly. 'Twas the most vile descent—shook me all to pieces.' There is no false bragging about that.

The ascent of Ben Nevis was still something of a feat. Even now there cannot be many who have composed a sonnet on his summit. There is a touch of bravado in the accomplishment; it is like smoking a pipe at 25,000 feet on the top of Kamet. Keats allowed himself very few such deeds. His whole acquaintance with mountains, we have said, was of tiny duration. But he was an active mountaineer in deed as well as spirit for all that, just as he was a describer of mountain scenery for all that he saw very little of it. The good Brown needed space—immense sheets of paper and pens in great number—to describe the beauties through which they passed on the way from Windermere to Keswick. As for Keats, he stopped a few moments to stand lost in wonder, to repeat 'How can I believe in that?' Then he went on, the thing seemed forgotten and he was soon talking about 'squashy holes'. But the mountains have remained, we shall meet them again:

> *Far, far around shall those dark clustered trees*
> *Fledge the wild ridgèd mountains steep by steep.*

He was a person, that is, for whom a very little mountain scenery could act like a slow spark, kindling at a later time. He did not need to be continually with it as Wordsworth did; and yet the phrases come flashing out at times as though he had known mountains all his life:

> *Or gazing on the soft new fallen mask*
> *Of snow upon the mountains and the moors.*

Even the mystery of rocks he sensed:

> *Crag jutting forth to crag, and rocks that seemed*
> *Ever as if just rising from a sleep.*

Or he would write descriptively in prose: 'These cloud veils opening with a dissolving motion and showing us the mountainous region beneath as through a loophole—these cloudy loopholes ever varying and discovering fresh prospect east, west, north and south.' Or we have that passage of 'Sleep and Poetry' which gives us to hope that he too, for all that 'the effect' of mountains may be 'wearing away', would place his final poetic crowning on their summit:

> *O Poesy, for thee I hold my pen,*
> *That am not yet a glorious denizen*
> *Of thy wide heaven,—should I rather kneel*
> *Upon some mountain top, until I feel*
> *A glowing splendour round about me hung . . .*

or the other passage, after a visit to Burns's country, where of the soul's memorial it is said:

> *He reads it on the mountain height, where chance he may*
> *sit down*
> *Upon rough marble diadem, that hill's eternal crown.*

Examining these passages we see why it was that he asked no Wordsworthianly long acquaintance with those heights. Keats saw, as Severn remarked, with greater vividness than anyone else. He stored the raptures of his visions and could then reproduce them, but without dumping them on our heads as object lessons. A sensualist, he was prepared to receive the impression and transmute it into poetry. True, he liked to 'humanize' hills, to relate them to men, but that was because he believed that humans were ultimately the more interesting. Quite early he wrote in a letter from Devon: 'Scenery is fine, but human nature is finer.' Thus the hills appropriately take on a personality. Mrs Cameron, in her epic encounter with Ben Nevis, is quite in keeping when she exclaims: 'Sweet Nevis, do not

quake.' And the Ben himself is made to bellow to his
henchman Red Crag (Carn Dearg):

> *Red Crag, there lies beneath my farthest toe*
> *A vein of sulphur. . . .'*

For this Ben is a person. He is a giant, in fact, upon whose
head the muse shall, in more serious vein, venture her
lesson, a prosy lesson enough about the mists which are in
the minds of men quite as present as upon the Scottish
cliffs. The impression of that mist clung to him, he did not
need long acquaintance with it. Herein too is the Keatsian
gift to the posterity of mountaineers. For there is in him
the idea of the *opposition* of man and Nature, their struggle
and the romantic feelings thereby inspired. This 'battle
with the giants' the moderns have continued to wage. Thus
to Keats the columns of Fingal's cave recall the mytho-
logical giants: 'Suppose now the giants who rebelled
against Jove had taken a whole Mass of black columns and
bound them together like bundles of matches, and then
with immense axes had made a cavern in the body of these
columns . . .' And because he likes humans, the hills and
lakes are peopled with human figures—Loch Lomond un-
fortunately with pleasure steamers, and its banks, he complains, with coaches which ought by all romantic rights to
give way to 'Barges with trumpets and Banners'. Or the
rough and lonely roads are walked by imaginary lords and
ladies: 'Sometimes when I am rather tired I lean rather
languishly on a rock and long for some famous Beauty to
get down from her palfry in passing, and approach me with
—her saddle bags, and give me—a dozen or two capital
roast beef sandwiches.' Such are the shapes of which the
sensualist dreams, which beckon him and with which he
would share the mountain spaces. These would be his
allies in the arduous task of standing up to Nature. The
letters written from the Scottish tour mention only once
the directly inspiring effect of hills upon a poet. The
walkers approached Ayr 'with a grand view terminated by

the black Mountains of the Isle of Arran. As soon as I saw them so nearly I said to myself "How is it they did not beckon Burns to some grand attempt at Epic?" ' For if Burns lived with that view before his window surely he had no excuse for not venturing, like Dante, 'l'un giogo di Parnasso'. Wordsworth would have agreed. But with Keats the thought is momentary. Left to himself, he reverts to the lowlands of Southern England for a permanent sojourn. He limits himself to the occasional in mountains; and wisely perhaps, for we have seen that long years spent in their company can be exhausting, and that both Dorothy and William were affected by them. Keats's pictures are the more vivid, their outline sharper to our sense as a background to witches, giants, dreamy poets or 'belles dames sans merci'. He shares the mountain lights that enliven the early, more playful Wordsworth; he cheers them with a sense of humour that William never possessed.

Therefore the mountains are for him a very small part of the whole picture, but they are a necessary part. They were necessary on the Scottish tour, if only because the romantic in him wanted time and space to adjust its ideas of Womankind. That will show up his idea of the mountains as playing a rôle towards himself, the man. Scotland was to 'give me more experience, rub off more prejudice, use to more hardship, identify with finer scenes, load me with grander mountains . . .', in short to make of him more the kind of person, the Romantic, that he would like to be. Mrs Wylie was given in August 1818 a newspaper account of 'a gentleman in a fur cap falling over a precipice in Kirkcudbrightshire'. She imagined that this must be John Keats. Alas no! 'Being half drowned by falling over a precipice is a very romantic affair', but he could not lay claim to such distinction. If only he were able—'no romance lady could resist me'. The precipice then formed a charming corner of the picture of the romantic person Keats aimed to be. Yet his 1818 tour, the one mountain

[101]

experience in that corner, was cut short by a sore throat.
If he had only lived longer, perhaps he would have come
back to become more orthodox. He might have lost the
sly, delightful laugh and written good solid mountain
poetry. But I think not. For he was one of those artists,
like Raphael and Mozart, who seem to have had something of such import to say that having said it—they die.
Almost we can see death shadowing them from the first; it
is not easy to imagine Keats 'settling down'. However in
one of the letters to Fanny Brawne of 1819 he thinks that
he would like to travel; Rousseau had made travel fashionable. 'Yet again, I am not so tired of scenery as to hate
Switzerland. We might spend a pleasant year at Berne or
Zürich.' We can never know what would have been his
impression of Switzerland and of its mountains; whether
we are wholly justified in a study of Keats among our
mountain persons at all, or whether he would have escaped
us, with a final chuckle, at the end.

John Ruskin and the Aesthetic Approach

The best image that the world can give of Paradise is in the slopes of the meadows, orchards and cornfields on the sides of a great Alp, with its purple rocks and eternal snows above.

IT would have been difficult for the prophet of 1810 to foretell the future of the newly reborn mountain love. He might have prophesied: 'Now that we have become acquainted with the mountains, now that we are no longer afraid of them and indeed are fascinated by them, the next step will be to clamber about their most secret recesses and work out the careful details of their rock crannies. We shall enjoy every new sensation that we can upon them, since those we know already are so good!' Or he might have said: 'Thus far and no farther. Enough that men have violated the sanctuary to this extent; from now on let us keep the mountains as the temple we have remarked them to be, and go no more prying into their holy of holies.'

In fact the trend of nineteenth-century thought took both these turns. It was the scientists, preceded by such as de Saussure, who first started breaking into the sanctuary.

They claimed that it was pure scientific ardour which set their feet on the snows of Mont Blanc, or Tyndall upon the summit of the Weisshorn. But it was more than this, as was proved by the event. They climbed also 'because they wanted to'. Those who came after the scientists and mingled with them, men like the founders of the Alpine Club, having made their scientific observations turn to the rapture of dawn and sunset, justify their new pursuit of mountaineering by the aesthetic pleasure, which the Victorians came to admit to be good, of sight and sensation.

On the other side the man whom we think of as one of the pioneers in that aesthetic movement, the man who in fact combined scientific and aesthetic, refused himself to enter at all into the sanctuary. Thus John Ruskin stands strangely alone and apart, in spite of the beauty of much that he has written. His followers in outlook, though not his followers to the hills, have been few, and his influence after the first enthusiasm was slight. Perhaps things would have been different had he come just a little later; at the time when he lay sketching under the Matterhorn, in the August of 1849, nobody had yet come near to climbing it —indeed it was to enjoy another sixteen years of privacy. As for the Chamonix Aiguilles which he so admired, they most certainly appeared in his day utterly impossible of ascent. A few years later he might have joined Whymper with his satchel and pencil slung over his knapsack; he might have followed the mountaineers instead of pouring his scientifically distilled cold water over their supposed acrobatics.

For after all, he had been from childhood up among hills and had enjoyed them. He had walked over Plynlymmon as a boy with his father; they were to be found 'getting up Cader Idris with the help of ponies; it remained, and rightly, for many years after, a king of mountains to me'. Or they climbed Snowdon, although he already adds the comment: 'I remember, as the most exciting event, the finding for the first time in my life a real "mineral" for myself, a piece of copper pyrites.' In fact in this chapter, 'Parnassus and Plynlymmon', of his *Præterita* he claims that he might have been the first geologist in Europe, had his parents only given him a Welsh guide, a Welsh pony and 'made a man' of him. They might too have made a mountaineer of him. There are many who spent early days among Welsh hills, who have gone out later to climb bigger mountains. And whatever Ruskin said afterwards, the idea of being up on very high places and not merely among them stuck with him. The clouds are more wonderful, he says, if you are above them. 'The mere power of familiarity with the clouds, of walking with them and above them, alters and renders clear our whole conception of the baseless architecture of the sky.' Or he even confesses that the process of a climb can have interest: ascending Monterone in Italy in 1858 he complains that it is the stupidest 'of all stupid mountains—grass all the way, no rocks, no interest'. Or he finds himself (earlier, in 1849) climbing avalanche debris near the Montanvers with Couttet (admittedly only in order to get a better view). The rocks were tricky. 'Awkward chasm between the ice and them; and at the only place where we could get upon them, another at the other side which made it a risk to pass the ridge. Got on to them at last, however. . . .'

But he was right perhaps when he said that his parents took him away and 'coddled' him. Herne Hill was a far cry from Chamonix, to which he was ever trying to prolong his visits, and the life of lecturer and writer did not seem to allow the time for mountain pleasures. Indeed even the periods of mountain business, when he was measuring angles or remarking the aesthetic values of the various rock forms, were snatched from the bosom of a family which suffered too patiently. The letters to Effie Gray show what kind of a man he could be in personal relationship; perhaps just because of this driving idea of 'business and a mission' on hill and plain to which all else must yield. He felt constrained, and by ill health into the bargain, to renounce the athletic pleasures. He comes even so early as 1861 to complain in a letter of his 'poor forty-two year old feet', which will scarce carry him up the path to Salève. If the wind got up, he confessed to his father two years later, when he was out for a stroll, it would put his temper out of control till next day. It was therefore 'strolling' which he enjoyed, the power to wander easily where one pleased, without the necessity of being confronted by Giant Difficulty. Thus he remarks, in the chapter of *Præterita* on the Col de la Faucille, that what he likes in the Jura is the liberty to wander far or near as you please, as it were on the Yorkshire moors. 'Among the greater hills one can't always go just where one chooses; all around is the too far or too steep.' To sum it up, he comes to the conclusion to which his own 'forty-two year old feet' may have helped to force him: 'The more I analysed, the less I felt able to deny the claims of prosaic . . . persons to be allowed to like the land level.'

Ruskin then may have been weaned by physical circumstance away from an early habit of scrambling to become a prophet of that other tradition, of which Fiona Macleod is a modern representative, which accuses us of using the mountains as a greased pole to our activity, of being too busy running up their sides, wherever we may most steeply find them, to stop and appreciate their beauty or return to awe of them. In *Modern Painters* he developed the idea: 'To get back to awe for hills, we must begin by divesting ourselves as far as may be of our modern experimental and exploring activity, and habit of regarding mountains chiefly as places for gymnastic exercise.' This is a prelude to the most important of his inconsistencies, for surely it is as much a sacrilege to regard them as scientific laboratories, and John Ruskin was nothing if not a scientist. A biographer claims that 'his descriptions of mountain

forms in *Modern Painters* are accounted by geologists the
most important of his contributions, or aids, to their
science'. Look only at his letter to Taylor, in 1875, on
receiving a drawing of the Binomial Curve of Mount
Sinai: '. . . it's all much too grand for and far away back
for me. I want to know how long the Staubbach has been
falling where it is in the valley of Lauterbrunnen. There is
a mere nutshell of a question for you geologists.' But no,
science and awe might be allowed to mix, not awe and
athletics.

And strangely enough the fathers of the Alpine Club
took the criticism meekly, perhaps because they were at
the same time unostentatiously slipping their own mountain activities past under the respectable mantle of science,
with aesthetics for her handmaiden. Leslie Stephen, in the
National Review of April 1900, begins by commending
Ruskin's accuracy of observation. Then:

> The fourth volume of *Modern Painters* infected me and other early
> members of the Alpine Club with an enthusiasm for which, I hope, we
> are still grateful. Our prophet indeed ridiculed his disciples for treat-
> ing Mont Blanc as a greased pole. We might well forgive our satirist,
> for he had revealed a new pleasure which we might mix with ingre-
> dients which he did not fully appreciate.

Not only did he not fully appreciate these, the physical and
sensual ingredients, he turned his back deliberately and
was inexorable in his denunciation of the mountaineers, or
indeed any who choose to spend their leisure among mountains at all. What do most of them visit the mountains
for? 'To get as fast as possible from place to place, and
secondly at every place where they arrive to get the kind
of accommodation and amusement to which they have been
accustomed in Paris.' Or in *Sesame and Lilies*: 'The Alps
themselves, which your own poets used to love so
reverently, you look upon as soaped poles in a bear-
garden, which you set yourselves to climb, and slide down
again with "shrieks of delight".' At the same time of
course he was indirectly stimulating the sport by his draw-

ings of the Matterhorn and the Chamonix Aiguilles; it
may even have been true of him, as Douglas Freshfield
wrote, that 'no writer has added so much to our enjoyment of Alpine scenery'. But openly and publicly he turned
his back.

We stumble here on another of the paradoxes. His purpose in writing was essentially practical. Science and
aesthetics never had human beings far behind them, and the
two chapters 'The Mountain Gloom' and 'The Mountain
Glory' of the fourth volume of *Modern Painters* introduce
the practical outcome of his studies: 'All the investigations
undertaken by me at this time were connected in my own
mind with the practical hope of arousing the attention of
the Swiss and Italian peasantry to an intelligent administra-
tion of the natural treasures of their woods and streams.'
Indeed he formed schemes of coming himself to help them
to relieve the 'Mountain Gloom'. This of course would
have to be done his way. He had reviled the Englishman
heartily enough, in *Sesame and Lilies*, for teaching the
Swiss 'the foulness of the modern lust for wealth, without
its practical intelligences'. But the Swiss have learned their
lesson their own way. The tourist industry, an 'adminis-
tration of natural treasures' *par excellence* is fifth in importance in the country. A great number of the tourists
are mountaineers and skiers—the latter perhaps the most
skilled experts of greased-pole technique. The Parsenn
Run and the Jungfrau Railway are the symbols of 'ad-
ministration'. Ruskin might have been horrified at his own
handiwork, at the learning of his lesson.

We must ask, then, what is the lesson of *Modern Painters*?
The fullest exposition of his views is to be found in the
two last chapters of Volume Four, and they are certainly con-
fusing. To begin with, he takes in his chapter on 'The
Mountain Gloom' the beautiful hills of Savoy. 'Here it
may well seem to the traveller, if there be sometimes hardship, there must be at least innocence and peace and fel-

lowship of the human soul with Nature. It is not so. . . . Enter the street of one of those villages and you will find it foul with that gloomy foulness that is suffered only by torpor, or by anguish of the soul.' He goes on to accuse the mountaineers of other disreputable qualities. The picture of their life is dark indeed, for the mountains inspire terror too. It is 'this mountain gloom, which weighs so strongly upon the human heart that in all time, as we have seen, the hill defiles have been either avoided in terror or inhabited in penance'. The Art of these men therefore is crude and their spirit crippled by bigotry.

We are walking, perhaps, in a summer afternoon up the valley of Zermatt . . . the snowy mountains shining like heavenly castles far above. We see, a little way off, a small white chapel . . . and we approach its little window, thinking to look through it into some quiet home of prayer; but the window is grated with iron . . . and behold— a heap of white human bones, mouldering into whiter dust.

Of course this is a criticism of the mountaineer only, not of his mountains. That appears soon enough from the chapter on 'The Mountain Glory'. Yet the jump needs something more of explanation than he will allow it. His human conclusion from natural beauty has been so very different from that of Wordsworth. Wordsworth saw hills to be lovely and exclaimed: 'How wonderful! Then those who live among the hills must have beautiful natures too!' Ruskin was moved to a reflection just the reverse. 'How strange that such human crudeness should dwell amid such beauty!' But he gives no sufficient reason why the Savoyards should be so ugly. Nor does he explain adequately why Dante's passage about the mountaineer should be taken as derogatory. It is surely the reverse. Shakespeare he will allow only to have appreciated the pine-tops in the mountain scene. But we know better. Indeed we suspect that 'The Mountain Gloom' has been inserted in part to give relish to the coming Glory (as well as to allow an attack on Romanism). 'I feared my own excessive love for them might lead me into too favourable interpretation of their

[109]

influence over the human heart. . . . For to myself mountains are the beginning and end of all natural scenery.' The whole chapter on the Glory follows this line of thought; as if he were trying to justify his own absorption in mountains in the face of all this weight of evidence that might be brought against him.

Thus all natural scenery for him is improved by hills, although he has at all times been careful to stress that these hills are best admired from below, not from their own tops. In *Sesame and Lilies*: 'The real beauty of the Alps is to be seen, and seen only, where all may see it, the child, the cripple, and the man of grey hairs.' Place a hillock on the flat plains of Normandy or Lincolnshire—the landscape is transformed. That is, it is transformed for him personally. But he goes on to discuss the mountains in literature and art. 'For this [literary power] the mountain influence is still necessary, only in a subordinate degree.' Mountains are admitted to be inspiring, but he denies that their inspiration is *necessary* to the greatest writers. The conclusions, we have seen, are unsatisfactory when we consider Dante and Shakespeare. But Art fares no better; the greatest artists were not inspired by mountains, and the art of the mountaineers is often, he says, grotesque and touched with horror. 'Michael Angelo, wholly an artist, and Raphael in later years, showed no love of mountains whatever.' Giotto, admittedly, Perugino and others 'use craggy or blue mountain distances'. But he does not explain this indifference if mountains can be to himself, as an artist, so clear a source of inspiration and affection. Nor does he reconcile this view with his theory that they so moved the sages and prophets through the ages that the hills of Sinai and Delphi, Monte Viso and Assisi, are associated for ever with the clearest in human vision. Ruskin, perhaps, had been carried too far by his own eloquence when he was writing of the Mountain Gloom. Or it may be that the mountains were too sacred even to be touched by human pen. Indeed it is the idea of sanctity which impresses itself upon the later part of the 'Glory' chapter. This quality may be defined in them under certain headings. First, they are obvious demonstrations of the idea of purpose in the Universe. 'Was all that granite sculpture and floral painting done by the angels in vain?' No, he sees too unmistakably a creating hand that made them. His study therefore is to be 'the subject of the sculpture of mountains into the forms of perpetual beauty which they have received from God'. He created them to be a lesson (here Ruskin too mounts a platform) upon certain themes. They teach the mutability of the earth and the mortality of everything upon it. The stream wearing at its stony bed upon Mont Blanc is a sign that even that mighty mountain range is falling, however slowly, to dust. Mountains are larger than we are, but they too die.

Secondly there is the lesson of mercy, though it is never clearly explained how this is taught. Had Ruskin experienced a thunderstorm in the high Alps his moral might have been different. But no, the mountains are merciful; it is the sea to which is assigned the quality of fierceness. 'The sea wave, with all its beneficence, is yet devouring and terrible; but the silent wave of the blue mountains is lifted toward Heaven in a stillness of perpetual mercy.' From these reflections follows the lesson of awe and simple piety. Simple in form themselves, the mountains were regarded, even in the Middle Ages, 'as bearing witness against the frivolity and luxury of the world'. As the obverse of this negative quality, they inspire the noblest and purest religious sentiments. The Deity has chosen them through all ages to be the symbol of human instruction. Apollo selected Delphi (Parnassus too, but literature has been excluded), as Jehovah chose Ararat and Mount Sinai. Later, in the Middle Ages, it was the monks who followed Christ's example and went up into high places. The conclusion is inevitable, that the anchorite alone has leisure and the right mental attitude to give thanks for these works and teachings of God. He best can sing praises.

But here is the old inconsistency. For what of the practical scientists, like Ruskin himself, or the hill dwellers whom he has been encouraging, in the 'Gloom', to take advantage of their natural resources? It is as if he looked with two eyes, and did not realize that one was out of focus with the other. He says in effect: 'To recover our awe for hills, to return to the monkish outlook, we must first of all rid ourselves of the "habit of regarding mountains chiefly as places for gymnastic exercise". We must not exert ourselves in activity among them.' At the same time he is an enthusiast for the scientific study of them. But physical science is just as much an 'activity' as mountain climbing; de Saussure and Tyndall showed that the two can be very profitably combined.

Finally he considers mountains a breeding ground for 'cults' and for many wrong kinds of worship. 'Much of the apparently harmful influence of the hills on the religions of the world is due to nothing else than their general gift of exciting the poetical and inventive faculties. . . .' He would have placed among those harmful religions that of the mountaineer, both climber and dweller. But if pure religion consists only of worship and contemplation, he must surely condemn also the scientist. For the scientist, if anybody, is concerned with the 'inventive faculties'. And a laboratory is quite as profane as a 'greased [or soaped] pole'.

These inconsistencies are perhaps one reason why Ruskin remained a voice crying in the wilderness. On the one hand he seems to say: 'Come up, be refreshed and recreated' (and he wrote himself, once, on returning to the hills after the plains: 'I had found my life again, all the best of it'); then when the worshippers come flocking to the glaciers he waves them sternly back. The glaciers are to be no soaped switchbacks; indeed he almost forgets the

The Cervin from the North-West Side

delight he had himself confessed in climbing among them. 'I don't know anything more wonderful in the Alps than this feeling of insufferable sunshine—with all the crevices in the snow filled with icicles.' Then again, even while he beckons them with one hand to the mountains as to the source of artistic and 'intellectual inspiration', with the other he waves them back, pointing to the miserable crudities of the mountaineers, or to the great poets and painters who were unaffected by hill scenery. He may have been unconsciously affected by the prevalent Victorian attitude to mountaineering. 'Prosperous security saw in it only a dangerous eccentricity', and Queen Victoria herself went so far as to suggest that it should be banned. Add the 'national mistrust of aesthetic or romantic sentiment' and we shall have Ruskin, anxious to slip his own aesthetics in under respectably scientific guise, an ardent champion in the forefront of the anti-mountaineers. Fiona Macleod and those naturalists who rove but do not attempt gymnastics might refuse to claim descent from him. They might point rather to the tourists he would so have scorned, who ascend to the Montanvers to click cameras and compare photographic results. These, they might say, are your disciples. But no, his contempt would have been too deep. Whatever he might allege of the hill dwellers, Ruskin does at heart throw in his lot with theirs. He has linked his fortune with the peasants whom he wished to encourage. Let us be generous, and hope that the old man of Coniston died at heart a mountaineer.

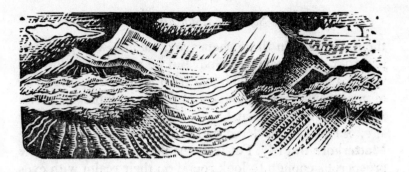

Leslie Stephen

> Climbing is a pleasure to me, and would be so if no
> one else climbed and no one ever heard of my climbing.

I T has been said that only when men have 'conquered'
Nature have they leisure to turn for aesthetic pleasure
to her mountains. Before that time the ranges are grim
barriers of inhospitable soil, harbourers of tempest and
symbols of infertility. Their inhabitants are the 'Alpine
Savages' of Horace Walpole's letters. But at last the plains
are tamed, industry is revolutionized to our use and even
the steep rocks boast their electricity-bearing streams,
their nooks of pasture and ploughland. It was now that
civilization could afford to produce Rousseau, with the
theory that these rocks are the symbol of savages who
were and are actually noble. Once we were like them, and
we must try again to become so. It could afford to allow
his ideas to strike deep, even while it smiled at his personal
preference for Nature 'paisible et riante'. The Wordsworths followed with a more active love of rugged places,
whose sternness they liked still to temper with human
habitation, with fields and hedgerows. For their mountains had a practical lesson for the men who dwelt among

[115]

them. To Ruskin these shapes and colours were an interpretation of the glory of God. But he refused to allow the
votaries inside: those who had tried to introduce the sport
of mountaineering stood convicted as temple breakers.
And we have seen that Queen Victoria, personifying her
age, seriously considered outlawing it altogether after the
Matterhorn tragedy. For it seems that the Victorians, now
prosperous enough to look round on their realm with eyes
for other than purely utilitarian advantage, were at first
strangely unwilling to do so. That realm of theirs was too
comfortable; why go sniffing at its spiky corners? A step
forward was taken when Edward Whymper's *Scrambles
Among the Alps* became popular; a further step when
mountaineering was made respectable through the com-
bination of literary feeling, humour and reverence which
went to Leslie Stephen's *Playground of Europe*.

It was the mixture of eccentricity and sound sense,
derived from his background and upbringing, which en-
abled Stephen to put his case so persuasively. He was sorely
needed to rescue his sport from being the pursuit only of
'academics and leisured intellectuals'. He slipped as a
young man, almost before he knew it, into a fellowship at
Trinity Hall, Cambridge, and the priesthood which this in
the year 1854 implied. He was physically frail before he
went to Cambridge, weaker than his brother Fitzjames,
who had been able to walk his thirty-three miles long
before Leslie started to walk at all. His parents thought
him unfitted for a strenuous career; that of fellow and tutor
in mathematics must have appeared ideally suitable. At
Cambridge he discovered to his own amused surprise that
he could perform physical feats of which he had never
dreamed. He could row—perhaps not well, yet adequately.
'A good oar he could never be', but he could coach. His
friend R. A. Bayford wrote that 'though a bad oar himself
he was a good coach'. Indeed just because he was a bad,
though energetic, oar, he was the more sympathetic with

the unproficient. 'I have never caught a cricket ball, and on the contrary have caught many crabs in my life.' The discovery of physical power flung him into the state of irrational and 'fanatical enthusiasm' for their sport which besets rowing gatherings, and which he bequeathed to the circle of the mountaineers. It was as if he were trying to make up for the years lost to Fitzjames. He not only rowed, he walked—and raced: two miles walking for instance against three miles running by Mr Thornton, 'later member for Clapham'. He raced along towpaths, over fields and hedges, along the road from Bedford to Cambridge. In 1855 the Alps appeared by chance over his horizon. It was these that he had needed to complete the picture.

There were three gaps which the mountains filled for him—physical, aesthetic and religious. The physical need was well and amply satisfied. In his first discovery of his own powers he had walked and raced without rest. Then he visited the Alps. He found himself in Austria in 1855, 'close up to a glacier, to my great satisfaction'. It was a small beginning. For that year and for many after he was at various centres, climbing the peaks which appear in the *Playground*. Half-ashamedly still, he confessed later, in his essay 'In Praise of Walking', that though his first enthusiasm for hills may have come in part from Ruskin, he could not keep up with 'the prophet's loftier teaching'. He could not restrain his legs from the summits. 'The influence of any cult depends upon the character of the worshipper, and I fear in this case the charm operated rather perversely. It stimulated a passion for climbing which absorbed my energies. . . .' In this matter of a physical complement, as necessary to spiritual appreciation, the influence of Stephen on the Victorian mind was most powerful. His white-hot enthusiasm for walking was infectious. Call it the working off of an inferiority complex in face of his brother Fitzjames, whom he found as the years went on increasingly antagonistic ('I am bound to say I disagree with his opinions more and more'); call it, if we will, the need to prove himself before a comfortable world. Men must be manly, he said, and women womanly. Be it named as it might, it was an urge absolute and irresistible to be physically active, no passive worshipper. But strangely, too, while he was in motion and exerting himself physically his mind became calmer and the desire to race left him. Dr Morgan, tried companion on the Eigerjoch, remarked of him that on the flats he appeared always to be seeking the greatest quantity of exercise possible in the time. It is in this character that he appears in George Meredith's *Egoist*. In the Alps on the other hand he adopted the guides' slow, unhurried step. He would not race, in theory at least, even if the description of him as 'fleetest of foot of all the Alpine brotherhood' breathes a faint odour of competition. 'Racing in the Alps is an abomination.' He spoke little at such times, and abhorred especially what he called 'gush'. According to himself he did not even think. 'Some people, I am aware, think while they walk . . .' (he had been guilty of the crime himself on the Sunday expeditions at home and in the essay on walking). For his own part, he found that there was nothing more soothing than the monotonous rise and fall of a pair of hobnailed boots. Increasingly, in the years after 1855, peace had come in the movement of two legs which his friends described as a pair of compasses.

He was sailing here, of course, directly across the Ruskinian guns. It was not wonderful that despite his admiration for Ruskin he should find his company trying. He wrote in a letter to Mr Norton in 1876, 'He makes, to say the truth, a very odd impression upon me. He regarded me with evident curiosity as, on the one hand, a specimen of the Alpine climbers whom he professes to detest. . . . For my part I could not be at ease with him.' At another time 'Mr Ruskin inflicts a scratch upon that complacent person, Mr Leslie Stephen, for saying that the Alps were improved by tobacco smoke'. Ruskin must inevitably have been put out of countenance by one who seemed to be setting up a gymnasium in one corner of his cathedral, and to be contaminating even that gymnasium with the weed. 'The Alps were for Stephen a Playground, but they were also a cathedral' (Douglas Freshfield). A cathedral in which a man might smoke, even if he could not think. When therefore Ruskin cried, in *Sesame and Lilies*, 'The French revolutionists made stables of the Cathedrals of France; you have made racecourses of the cathedrals of earth', it was these fathers of the Alpine Club that he was addressing. But Stephen had committed before Ruskin a yet huger crime. He dared to treat mountains and mountaineering with humour, a humour indeed essential if his compatriots were to be persuaded that the sport, *qua* sport, was worth pursuing. It must have as little useful aim or object as cricket. He therefore pours direct and jocular scorn upon the scientists and the utilitarians, upon all those who affect to visit hills for purposes hygienic or meteorologic, for any reason rather than the right one. 'Upon the summit of the Rothorn, "and what philosophical observations did you make?" will be the inquiry of one of those fanatics who, by a reasoning process to me utterly inscrutable, have somehow irrevocably associated Alpine travelling with science.' Himself, on the contrary, he relates that he never could use his brain above 5,000 or so feet, and that he once took Hume with him to the Alps, only to fail to read a word of him. He makes light, therefore, of the earnest seekers. He goes on to personify, humorous fashion, the very mountain shapes of Ruskin's 'Glory' in a manner, to Ruskin's way of thinking, highly unbecoming. They are monsters, often enough, behaving 'in a strangely capricious manner', crouching as if to pounce on the traveller or nodding friendly at evening. On Mont Blanc, 'the icy jaws of the great mountain seem to be enclosing

you in a fatal embrace'. It was not by chance that Thomas
Hardy in his sonnet likened Stephen himself to the rugged
Schreckhorn, perhaps the finest peak of which he had made
the first ascent. Then the figures of men among the mountains, the guides for instance, these too appear in mantles
of humorous description. There was never a doubt of
Stephen's opinion of their skill and courage. The Alpine
Club received in submissive silence his verdict that the
best amateur could never be the equal of a third-rate guide.
But having delivered this dictum, he was prepared to poke
fun at his beloved leaders, to build humorous personalities
around them as one might round the heroic Dr Grace. We
share his fretful impatience at Peter Michel, munching his
interminable bread and cheese and meat under the chilly
Schreckhorn in the early hours. We smile with him at the
nervous Herr Pfarrer on the Bietschorn, or pour scorn
with Lauener when he mounts the most dangerous-looking
ice pinnacle in sight to send forth screams before the horrified Chamonix guides, who had feared that a whisper
might bring the masses tumbling about their ears. It is a
literary humour too, well bred and never vulgar, even in
its outbursts. It is familiar with Dante, who would have
reserved the wind-swept ridge of the Rothorn for the faith-
less guides, or it can discourse interestingly and with a
wealth of reference, in the 'Old School' and the 'New
School', of dragons and priests and poets among the mountains. It is such humour as Ruskin could never have understood; for it is the humour of the sportsman, of the 'fanatical enthusiast' who, by the very lightheartedness of his
enthusiasm for a 'mere' pastime, touches near to the British
heart.

Stephen found an aesthetic satisfaction beside the physical.
He was no technical aestheticist. He might have become a
judge of pictures, he says, had he followed Ruskin further.
As it was he only became a pretty good judge of an Alpine
guide. Aesthetic appreciation entered his mountain view

The Schreckhorn and Finsteraarhorn

not as a weapon justifying his sport but added as it were
in afterthought, in the manner of Englishmen. In the two
essays especially, 'A Bye Day in the Alps' and 'Sunset on
Mont Blanc', he gives an analysis of sensation. On the
Dent d'Oche above Evian he describes the detail both of
the physical climb and the rest on the summit, with the
'Sybarite's couch' of delicious repose thrown in halfway
up. He analyses the method by which he wins most pleasure
from the scenery. At the top he lies flat on the ground.
'That, I will venture to say, is an excellent way of enjoying grand scenery. You should not look at external
objects, but feel that you could look at them if you were
not too lazy.' He tries therefore to become a part with the
scene, 'an animated top of the mountain', in a kind of
Buddhist Nirvana. He is right, that this is the most satisfying approach. He is right too that it should be made by
a man without companions. But unlike the bona fide
anchorite, or indeed the complete aesthete, he is forced
down along 'the now prosaic high road'. The Englishman
does not linger upon the heights, whether of fancy or fact,
too long without a laugh. He returns to his dinner. So it
is too at the end of 'The Regrets of a Mountaineer'. He has
discussed the question, whether the mountains are best
appreciated from below. 'People are always demonstrating
that the lower views are the most beautiful', but he has
argued that the mountaineer is the one diner at Nature's
table who is qualified to speak about that. He has sampled
all the dishes and vintages, and the mountains are the
champagne which he alone has tasted. He can measure and
compare them, he can enjoy the sensations so manifold
which make up experience on their surface. Stephen's own
descriptions of summit scenery are a sufficient justification
of his theories. But he ends again here, and even in that
best of all mountain pictures, the 'Sunset on Mont Blanc',
with the humorous reminder that we are, after all, for all
our exalted moments, no more than comical worm-like

creatures. No glory of the sunset can alter that fact. 'One is still of the earth, earthy; for freezing toes and snow parched noses are lively reminders that one has not become an immortal.' Or in 'The Alps in Winter', where the strain has verged upon the lyrical and where he has come, describing the familiar faces seen under unfamiliar coating, the nearest that he ever came to purple: 'But I am verging upon the poetical. Within a few hours we are again struggling for coffee in the buffets of railway stations.'

Besides physical and aesthetic satisfaction Stephen found among the hills a basis of worship. This too he has transmitted to later generations. We have seen that he slipped into the fellowship and priesthood at Cambridge. During the years following 1854, many doubts presented themselves. It was the reading of the lessons in chapel, 'those dubious stories', that first worried him. Then he was dissatisfied with his complacent colleagues, 'quite indifferent to high church and low church controversies, but somehow comfortably and complacently accepting the thirty-nine Articles in a lump without asking awkward questions'. The doubts simmered inside him until they burst their way out in a resignation of his tutorship in 1862 and a final departure from Cambridge three years later. They are touched upon, but only lightly, in his *Sketches of a Don at Cambridge*, set out at length in *An Agnostic's Apology*. They left him without a religion. 'My faith in anything like religion is growing dimmer. I can scarcely believe that two and a half years ago I was still reading prayers as a parson.' He was not cynical or bitter about this change from what Mr Kelly had described as his 'muscular Christianity'. He had resigned himself to it. But at the same time were come the Alps, to supply at any rate the cathedral for something that should fill the gap. He writes of them often enough as sacred places in the *Playground*, but we remember his lurking smile. Even so, as an oarsman, had he done comical reverence to his oar. But the bend in the path near Täsch, where he once met his future wife, Miss Thackeray, is described as 'sacred'. Wengern Alp is 'sacred': 'To me the Wengern Alp is a sacred place —the holy of holies in the mountain sanctuary . . . Byron's exploitation of the scenery becomes an impertinence.'

Despite the smile, then, he was at heart solemn enough. In fact hills were almost too sacred to write about— certainly too sacred for conversational 'gush'. It is with many an apology that he prefaces the *Playground*: 'With my eyes open to the weakness of my conduct I do what I have often condemned in others, and make a statement which I might more wisely have left to my enemies'. But once he has launched into it, the reality of his worship shines through the façade of 'shop'. Here at any rate, in the Alps, is an elevating and stimulating spirit, which recalls the best in us each time that we see them. Meaner things are forgotten, the disagreements with Fitzjames or doctrinal controversy. 'The trifling and vexatious incidents cannot adhere to such mighty monuments of bygone ages. They retain whatever of high and tender and pure emotion may have once been associated with them.' 'If I were to invent a new idolatry (rather a needless task) I should prostrate myself, not before beast, or ocean, or sun, but before one of those gigantic masses to which, in spite of all reason, it is impossible not to attribute some shadowy personality.' Thus the mountains are, as it were, larger but more definite creations than ourselves, links between man and whatever power is responsible for us all. Their very design posits a designer. The Jungfrau: 'A chaos of grand forms, it yet suggests some pervading design, too subtle to be understood by mortal vision, and scorning all comparison with earthly architecture.' He is very near here to the design argument for a God or Creative Power. But his mountains never answer him who their Creator is. 'At Stonehenge we ask what human beings could have erected these strange grey monuments, and in the mountains we instinctively ask what force can have carved out the Matterhorn, and placed the Wetterhorn on its gigantic pedestal.' We ask, but we do not answer. Indeed, those who have turned from doctrinal Christianity are unlikely to find answers, or anything but further question marks. Stephen has been accused, and by his own biographer, of being 'impure' in his love of mountains, in reckoning their inspiration, for example, more valuable than that of the poets and prophets. He had erected the cathedral, 'but nobody worships a cathedral'. Perhaps that is true; but at least an Unknown God is a better inhabitant of so dignified an edifice than a God in whom a man has ceased in his heart of hearts to believe. Stephen was to the end an agnostic, ever yearning back towards some semblance of the Creator he had rejected.

Virginia Woolf, in a memoir of her father, has pictured the years of his old age. He could climb no more, he could do no better than 'potter', a word which meant a more strenuous exertion for him than for most men. He would still stride for hours alone across the Cornish moors, as in the days when Meredith had described him as 'Phoebus Apollo turned fasting friar'. There are two especially interesting details in her picture: his relation to his children and his sympathy for his fellows. He would not allow the girls to smoke cigarettes, because he did not approve of smoking as a female habit, but he gave them an absolute freedom in their choice of career. They might even become painters, although 'he had no special love for painting'. They might, that is to say, do anything so long as it conformed to certain standards of behaviour which Stephen had set up for himself. 'Freedom of that sort was worth thousands of cigarettes.' And for his fellows: he felt a sympathy even for remote peoples, something like that which used to beset Lowes Dickinson. He would lie awake at night during the South African war picturing the

[124]

wounds and the suffering. Or nearer home, 'neither his reason nor his common sense helped to convince him that a child could be late for dinner without having been maimed or killed in an accident'. These two qualities in him were the gift of the mountains: toleration and sympathy. Just because he had arrived at no hard and fast religious dogma, he allowed and even asked on behalf of others the latitude which he demanded for himself. The mountains gave that freedom, as they gave the belief that there was a significance in the world, such as to make freedom or its reverse important questions. And if toleration, then sympathy. Before these 'gigantic masses', as before their Creator, we are all equally insignificant. We must sympathize with those other poor creatures condemned to the same lot as ourselves, we must behave towards them according to a certain code of humane conduct, not because it is ordained from above, but because it is natural for all of us, circumstanced together as we are, to feel and own it. This is an inconclusive philosophy, it may be said. Stephen owned up to its inconclusiveness with a smile. He pointed often to his own unsatisfactory career, 'jack of all trades and master of none'. He might have promised that with another fifteen years' hard thinking he would work through to something more satisfactory. But at least it was a code which made for peace, for the happy if happy-go-lucky life. His countrymen could adopt it in a clear consciousness of brotherhood. 'Les montaignes sont à tout le monde.'

Nietzsche and Modern Mountaineering

Herz hat, wer Furcht kennt, aber Furcht zwingt, wer
den Abgrund sieht, aber mit Stolz.

F RIEDRICH NIETZSCHE has been blamed for many
excesses of modern days. It would be hard upon
him if we were to charge him also with the corruption
of mountaineering morals between the wars. Yet he in-
fluenced, even in their attitude to the hills, a greater
number of persons than his contemporary, Leslie Stephen.
If Hitler is the political outcome of his doctrine of Superman, then his children without a doubt in the realm of
physical activity are the brothers Schmidt and the 'con-
querors' of the Eiger Nordwand, or the Frey brothers
who on the Watzmann refused at first to answer their
rescuers' signals, still believing in their ability to do the
climb or willingness to die upon it. We must look more
closely then at Nietzsche to trace a line between the frail
German professor of Classics and the bronzed 'tigers' who
flaunted their hammers and slings through the streets of
Grindelwald.

At the time when Leslie Stephen was writing his *Playground* Friedrich Nietzsche was still at his studies. As a

young man he was physically energetic and had for some
time before 1868 entertained the idea of joining the Army;
he joined, and showed himself an active and enthusiastic
soldier until the accident occurred which he describes in a
letter: 'One day I failed in attempting a smart spring into
the saddle. I gave my chest a blow on the pommel and felt
a sharp rend in my left side.' He continued his duties, however, without saying anything, until weakness compelled
him to be medically examined. Probably this injury perma-
nently affected his health. It was followed by an illness
which weakened him further. He had been elected professor
of Basle University at an extremely early age. In 1870
came the Franco-Prussian war. Nietzsche, living in
Switzerland, was not allowed to take part as a combatant.
He went to the war as a volunteer in an ambulance unit,
and contracted dysentery and diphtheria nursing the
wounded. He never recovered full health. Indeed from this
time he became, not hypochondriac, but gently vale-
tudinarian, one who could almost boast the complaint of
'nerves'. His spirits were affected easily by meagre
attendances at his lectures. Wagner's music 'tortured him
for six years', until their friendship broke. In 1879 he was
compelled on health grounds to resign his professorship;
the remaining years of his intellectual life, before his brain
gave way, he passed in Italy, at Nice, but most especially
in the Engadine, which he came to regard as a haven:
'Now I know a nook where I can gain strength, work with
fresh energy'. He lived the life his health demanded; he was
taking, in 1881, '5–7 hours moderate exercise a day', with
a sparing diet whose main ingredient was aniseed biscuit.

. . . . .

We would not expect such a man to exercise himself
actively among mountains. He looked for solitude in which
to write and think, even while he realized that this solitude
was dangerous, that it stretched too tightly the rope

[128]

The Eigar North Wall

between genius and insanity. 'We solitary ones, how dangerously do we live!' He did not therefore ask for physical exertion but rather repose from hills. The most he was prepared for was to walk with the multitude along their highways. In 1872, on the way towards Italy, he visited Chur in Switzerland. From Chur he did the 'Splügen tour' by diligence:

> The finest diligence drive I have ever had. . . . It made me feel as if I did not yet know Switzerland at all. This is my Nature. . . . This high Alpine valley (5,000 feet) is exactly to my taste—pure and bracing air, hills and rocks of every shape and size, and mighty snow mountains all around. But what I like most of all are the magnificent high roads along which I can walk for hours at a time, without heeding the road in the least.

The words describe the physical exertions of many a myriad tourists. 'Mountains and woods are better than towns'; a sentiment echoed by every protégé of Thomas Cook who finds himself for the first time marvelling at the Matterhorn from the Gornergrat. Many a tourist too has written upon his picture postcard sentences like that addressed to Madame Louise von O: 'I shall not forsake my mountain loneliness without once more writing to tell you how fond I am of you.' It was not then through his own performance that Nietzsche pointed the way to Superman.

The Nietzsche who begat Superman is Zarathustra. That strange composite being, hero of the work (*Thus Spake Zarathustra*) composed in the early years after his retirement from Basle, can voice the thoughts and perform the feats which his timid creator dreamed but did not dare. He can protest against the comfortable assurance of an age to which Nietzsche's lectures had tasted too thorny, in words that Nietzsche had himself used, but in private letters only. 'Read Shakespeare: he is full of [such] men, raw, hard and mighty men of granite. Our age is so poor in these men!' The writer himself could not be called one of them. But Zarathustra, who descends at times from his mountain cave to associate with humans and to give them the benefit of his counsel, can elaborate this theme just because he is himself possessed of strength. He scorns women, not because, like Nietzsche, he is unacquainted with them and afraid of them, but from a full knowledge. He rejoices in the strong, not the womanish. The strong, he says in the first book, are as the highest stones of the mountain pyramid; these are exposed, because of the glory of their position, to the most violent wind, the keenest cold, the hottest sun. It was for them, the strong, that the very bases of those hills were built, that they might support the towering splendour of the summit rocks.

It interests us that Nietzsche should also associate the mountain tops with the loneliness of the great. He recalls another pessimist, Alfred de Vigny, sending his Moses up a mountain to complain before God of his isolation. For he too knows that this solitude is not a happy thing, it is a thing of 'Sehnsucht', of longing that can never be quenched. 'Alas, where shall I now ascend with my longing? From all the mountain tops I look out for my father's and my mother's lands.' Yet Zarathustra cannot keep his feet from the heights. At the beginning of the third book, the most significant for mountain symbolism, he sets out once more to climb the hill. 'I like not the plain.' This hill is associated for him with danger and discipline equally with loneliness. If man is, as elsewhere described, 'the rope to Superman', he is also a 'rope over a precipice'. Thus is the idea of danger linked with the soaring steep summits. 'Not the height, the declivity is the terrible thing. The declivity where the glance hurleth down and the hand graspeth up. There the heart becometh dizzy for its double will.' In the later chapter, 'Of the Vision and the Riddle' there is difficulty also apparent in this ascent of the strong: the difficulty of mounting up over stones that drag down; 'striding silently over the scornful rattling of pebbles, crushing with its step the stone that made it slip, thus my foot forced its way upward'. That is to say, the hero must ascend in defiance of the spirit that pulls down. There is discipline and concentration demanded by the effort to climb high, to see much. This discipline is all of a piece with the Nietzschean theory that suffering, itself bad, may yet be productive of good. 'The discipline of suffering—of *great* suffering, know ye not that it is only this discipline that has produced all the elevation of humanity hitherto?' And again: 'This hardness is requisite for every mountain climber.' Or a little later, in the 'Wanderer' of the third book, he returns to and amplifies the association of greatness with the act of climbing upward over a hazardous path: 'Thou goest the way of thy greatness. Thy best courage must now be that behind thee there is no further path. Thou goest the way of thy greatness. Thy foot itself extinguished the path behind thee, and above it there stands written "Impossibility".'

The reward for him who has so climbed is the achievement of Superman. Nietzsche's hero is at times dangerously near to the mountaineer quoted by C. G. Jung, who dreamed that he was climbing with ease upward and ever up, and fell to his death some weeks later through making a step on to a hold that did not exist. 'Alas,' says Zarathustra, 'I have grown weary of their highest and best. From their height I longed to rise upwards, out, away to Beyond-man.' At the summit itself he is rewarded by a view of the sea. 'Out of the greatest depth the highest must rise to the height.' But he is not satisfied even with his summit. What he has really longed for is elevation even to the sky, the bright clear sky that is the crown of it all. In 'Before Sunrise' Zarathustra sings:

When I wandered alone,—for what did my soul hunger in nights and labyrinthine paths? And when climbing mountains,—for whom did I ever search except for thee upon the mountains?

All my wandering and mountain climbing was only a necessity and makeshift of the helpless one. Flying is the only thing my will willeth, —flying into thee.

Typically, Zarathustra discounts and even dislikes clouds, prime source of mountain beauty. 'Whom could I hate more than wandering clouds? . . .' They are shadowy, indeterminate creations that obscure the hardness of the heroic outline. But as we are beginning to see, he is really no lover of the mountains themselves. He finds them, like man, a 'rope' to the Heaven where Superman reigns. For men themselves, as he says and as Nietzsche maintained always, are divided into the strong and the weak, those whose proper function is to rule and for whom the world was made, and those apt only for the 'slave morality'. Christianity fosters this slave morality. Zarathustra will not therefore, like Christ, be merciful; he will be stern: 'I show them only the ice and winter on my summits—and not that my mount tieth around itself all the girdles of the sun.' With the metaphor of the sun he ends: 'Thus spake Zarathustra and left his cave, glowing and strong, like the morning sun which cometh from dark mountains.'

This book, itself a difficult, a rambling and poetical out-pouring, gives in its oracular utterances the clue to much of the Continental mountain philosophy in the period be-tween the wars. Mountaineering practice has proceeded by phases. We have seen at first Leslie Stephen and the epoch of guided climbing, when the guideless would scarce dare to show themselves within the portals of the Alpine Club. Towards the end of the century, both from preference and financial need, the habit of guideless climbing took root, but with the accent still on safety. The main ridges of the main peaks of the Alps were ascended by moun-taineers like Geoffrey Winthrop Young and his friends, climbing with and without guides. In the later phase of between the wars the British climbers on the whole kept to the tradition of Leslie Stephen. The Continental 'tigers' climbed to a larger extent than the British without guides, and looked round desperately for what had not yet been achieved. They are driven on to the faces: the Watzmann in winter, the Italian Drei Zinnen, the Grandes Jorasses and the northern wall of the Eiger. These faces they climb with infinite danger and difficulty by means of a battery of iron pegs, ropes and hammers. Many lives have been lost in the attempts. The greater part were made by the Germanic peoples inspired by Hitler; some of the hardest Dolomite routes are the prize of Italians, under the aegis of Mussolini. If we look at certain common features of the new school we shall find ourselves curiously back with Nietzsche and the airy longings of Zarathustra.

Let us first be chary of the idea that these feats were done in the hope of material reward. It is true that some climbs were done simply in the hope of a job. Honours were certainly heaped on the 'victors' of the most arduous ascents, and they were fêted in triumphal celebrations on their return; yet reward and celebrity were never the main motive of these enterprises. Rather, C. F. Meade has written, 'the strange heroes who perform these feats are sometimes dismayed by the glaring publicity in which they find themselves involved', and seek to fly back, like Zarathustra, to their solitude.

A significant article appeared in the *Swiss Alpine Club Journal* for 1948, entitled 'Der Bergsteiger Friedrich Nietzsche'. Herr Sepp Walcher, of Vienna, quoting and amplifying the passages of Nietzsche which typify mountain aspirations, has this to add of his own: 'But they become lonely, the solitary ones among the many. They find fewer and fewer brothers and sisters.' He has just given us Nietzsche's: 'Ever fewer climb with me up ever higher mountains', and it must be our conclusion that these modern mountaineers too prefer their lonely retreat. One reason for that preference is that their view of common human life is at bottom deeply pessimistic. In this they resemble their master Nietzsche. They are affected with 'a contempt for life so deeply buried in the unconscious mind that no pessimism or despair betrays itself on the surface,

[133]

save when it leads to the perpetration of deeds such as these'. It was typical of two Bavarians before an attempt on the north face of the Morgenhorn, which was to prove fatal, that they should have said: 'For us Germans there is nothing more to lose.' Nietzsche too was a pessimist. His master had been Schopenhauer. Zarathustra believed, like the young Bavarians, in 'a passion for self-destruction', since only by destroying or escaping from self was it possible to win the heights. His saying had been: 'In order to see much it is necessary to forget oneself.'

We have seen that the idea of danger as an ingredient of the full life was never far from Nietzsche's thought, and that even in private letters he refers to the danger of the lonely ones. The element of risk was of course a 'sine qua non' of German climbing between the wars, and linked curiously with the Nietzschean theory of the perfect man. Fear in danger is necessary, for it is the overcoming of fear that brings the good. Under his heading 'Gefahr und Furcht' Herr Walcher gives the quotation: 'He has a heart who knows fear, but he overcomes fear who sees the precipice, but is undaunted.' He adds of his own: 'We will be stronger than fear, greater than danger, we will master both of them, because we know that every conquest is a step towards perfection.' And he is echoed by an Italian climber who described his climbing, between the wars, as 'a struggle of the will against the baseness of fear and instinct; a proof and consciousness of our spiritual power; an affirmation of faith in ourselves and our life'.

Thus this conquest of fear is necessary to Superman's evolution, and with the *future* of Superman Nietzsche is really concerned. To him rather than to persons of our own generation we owe love, allegiance, loyalty. 'I teach you Beyond-man. Man is something that shall be surpassed; what have ye done to surpass him?' So too, in works like Fritz Bechtold's *Nanga Parbat Adventure*, we learn, at the conclusion, that just by dying gloriously in their struggle with the mountain dangers, the German climbers laid the way for future mountaineers. 'Splendid as it must be to return home with the prize of this mighty mountain, it is yet nobler that a man lay down his life for such a goal, to be a way and a light for the young hearts of those that come after.' Dying then is glorious, if it is for such a cause and if Providence wills it. (Of course at other times Providence may will the other way. One of the Germans on the Eigerwand in 1935, when bad weather was threatening to end the assault, said: 'It almost looks as if Providence wants to preserve us from death.' Death itself did not matter so long as the climbers were prepared to face its possibility.)

Now according to Nietzsche, as we have seen, men must be prepared to suffer as well as to die if they wish their kind to win through to a higher state. This idea is cardinal to his theory. Suffering is usually considered an evil; in fact it is a means to good, he says, because it brings out fine qualities which would otherwise lie hidden. Nobody could accuse the modern Continental climbers of shirking suffering. They seek it, rather, again and again, as the only way of proving manhood. In this tone Paul Bauer, the greatest mountaineer perhaps of his generation, wrote after the magnificent but unsuccessful attempt on Kangchenjunga:

> We needed some means of proving that he who was dauntless and undeterred, he who was prepared to make the highest sacrifice, and he alone, could aspire to the highest attainment. Defiantly resisting the spirit of that time, we had to show again and again what these virtues could achieve in spite of the heaviest odds.

In one feature indeed the new cult appears un-Nietzschean: its nationalism. This may be the symptom of more modern beliefs superimposed upon the old. It is studied at length by R. L. G. Irving in *The Romance of Mountaineering*, and he quotes from an Italian journal the practical justification for international rivalry: 'All our wars will always take place in the mountains.' In order to encourage the habit of performing difficult feats in mountain country, 'the medal for valour in sport, the highest distinction accorded by the Duce to exceptional athletes . . . will be awarded to climbers who vanquish mountains by new ascents of sixth standard'. Indeed the Government sent a telegram of condolence to the relatives of a climber killed on the Grandes Jorasses, because he had 'died on the field of honour'.

This development would not have pleased Nietzsche any better than a specifically German Hitler. Yet so far he would have been in agreement: the strong should rule (Hitler would have added that only the Germans could be called strong). His definition of strength is fullness of life. Zarathustra, in a striking speech about the Reversed Cripples, taunts the 'ear, an ear as great as a man', from whose stalk hung a 'poor little bloated soul', which the folk told him was a man of genius. But Zarathustra knew that it was a Reversed Cripple. Only one organ of the whole body was really formed. Life, the power to live and to enjoy fully, is what he demands. He does not try to answer the objection (put, for instance, by A. C. Pigou) that 'mere quantity of life does not present itself to our consciousness as the only good thing'. And following his thought the climbers between the wars asked for life, for 'strength through joy' and for abundance, for a 'love of living' that should enable the suffering necessary to the highest experience. We may quote again Herr Walcher, under his heading 'Lust und Leid': 'Joy and suffering are the pulse-beat of life. They alone give to all experience height, depth and content.' There is a certain naïvety corresponding to Nietzsche's in this uncritical demand for life in bulk. It corresponds too to the Germans' voluntary political blinkering. They did not want to ask why. In a book published at Munich in 1940 Ernst Grob (himself a Swiss) gives an account of a Swiss-German ascent of the very difficult Tent Peak in the Sikkim Himalaya. 'A wild desire seizes us to begin the struggle with this giant. We do not ask after the reason, we do not ask questions about existence or non-existence. We have fallen completely under the charm of the mountains. To experience—that is enough for us' (Ernst Grob, *Drei in Himalaja*).

Nietzsche then had influence in a sphere which he little suspected; for mountaineering was in its infancy when he wrote. He died, unconscious and with his reason gone. The political philosophy which he transmitted to two dictators seemed in 1945 to have crashed with them to ruins. Whether it has really disappeared remains still to see. But the mountain cult which he unknowingly inspired is most certainly not dead, nor maybe will it ever die so long as that pessimism which is born of unsuccessful wars persists. It is for the future mountaineer to attempt a reconciliation between the love of full living, which is good, and the considerations of humanity which require a balance in all things. Life is a mixture of the elements, a mixture that must be nicely adjusted. For it was another Swiss, Ernst Grob's brother, who wrote in preface to the mountain adventure:

> *For Life is a song that beats and thrills,*
> *Giving and taking, sacrifice and theft,*
> *A tasting to the full and a denial;*
> *And beyond suffering there lies, somewhere,*
> *The calm of reconciliation.*[26]

[26] Da ist das Leben ein wirbelndes Lied,
   Ein Nehmen und Schenken, ein Rauben
   Und Opfern, ein Auskosten und Entsagen;
   Und über allem Leid liegt irgendwo
      Immer eine stille Versöhnung.

The Religious View and Pope Pius XI

May God, who dwells on the heights, bless the expedition.

I T has appeared already that the mountains both
stimulate and satisfy religious enthusiasm. This question Ruskin studies in some detail, in an interesting but
confused section of the fourth volume of *Modern Painters*.
The monkish view, he says (and it is the view which he
most of all admires), is based on the Latin Vulgate. The
mountains most immediately concerned are Ararat, where
the Ark found rest, Sinai and that Mount upon whose
summit Jesus Christ was tempted of the Devil. 'It seemed
then to the monks that the mountains were appointed by
their Maker to be to man Refuges from Judgement, signs
of Redemption, and altars of Sanctification and Obedience.'
Therefore the deaths of Aaron and Moses and the 'assump-
tion of office' by Christ were linked symbolically with
heights. From that time hill areas have taken their place
as a temple, and hill scenery as a powerful stimulus to
religious enthusiasm. At the same time he criticizes 'im-
purity' of devotion. 'The faith of enthusiasm is apt to be
impure, and the mountains, by exciting morbid conditions

of the imagination, have caused in great part the legendary and romantic forms of belief.' On these grounds he condemns the bigotry and distorted worship of the Savoyards, or the wealth and worldliness of the Vatican. These are contrasted with the pure devotion of the persecuted Covenanter. In Ruskin's view, then, enthusiasm for mountains is necessary and beneficial, unless it is being exploited by some section of the Church of Rome.

The utterances of the Fathers of our Faith upon this cornerstone of their Creed have ever been impressive. After Sinai and Ararat the Psalmist, with his expectation of help from over the mountain ridge. Then the Anchorites, whom Ruskin praises, with justice, for the purity of their emotion. And alongside these the Fathers of the Church, like St Augustine, whose words read by Petrarch upon the summit of Mont Ventoux struck home so appropriately: 'Men go abroad to admire the heights of mountains and the long winding courses of rivers, the compass of the ocean and the courses of the stars, and themselves they forget.' It was small wonder that this passage filled him with humility and repentance for his own supposed falling from the way. He was not extraordinary in this. It is only his greater sensitivity and power of expression that pick him out. How many through the ages have inherited his view, have supposed the mountains to teach both the calm of acquiescence and the omnipotence and artistry of their Creator!

This might fairly be denied of the early eighteenth century. For the eighteenth century disliked this 'Uniformity of Barrenness', perhaps just because a number of its most intelligent minds lacked that sense of awe which the mountains had hitherto inspired. They felt uncomfortable when ushered into a Higher Presence. But we have seen that the stream was trickling on, to burst its dams towards the end of the century. What we have now to ask is how far the Creator of the mountains returned to be worshipped along with and above them; that is to say, how far the men of religion, in contrast to disappointed agnostics like Leslie Stephen, still lifted up their eyes to a God above the hills. And how far might their whole view of that God be tinted by the spectacles through which they looked at the mountains? Let us choose then a man of modern times, a theologian. Let us see whether he in our day experienced those twin sensations of wonder and humility, whether he too saw in mountains the props to desired belief and spurs to noble action. His name shall be Achille Ratti, who became later Pope Pius XI.

Achille Ratti's father was the manager of a silk factory at Desio in North Italy. The son acquired his love of rambling early among the neighbouring hills. He began to find in the mountains the pleasure of an escape into the romantic world which became later a necessity to imprisoned librarian and priest. 'The ramble', his biographer says, 'might enable him to discover little romances of fact and form personal to himself, such as a new method of approaching a familiar climb.' His rambling also confirmed the natural placidity of his temperament: 'His even temper was a byword among the village boys.' He loved 'climbing and reading', and being scholarly by nature he came very early to associate the two, so that his accounts later of his climbs show the patience in observation and thoroughness in research of a well-read scientist. A scientist he could have become, had he turned his thoughts in that direction.

Instead he entered the Theological Seminary at Milan in 1876, at the age of nineteen. One important difference between this type of seminary and English educational institutions was that the seminary cut out that broader side of our education too often covered by the one word 'games'. Ratti was free to associate himself with some Swiss enthusiasts and devote his time to study, with the occasional walk and hill climb as his only relaxation. Small

wonder if the hills became in his imagination increasingly
the magical scenery against which theological research took
place. They posed exactly the same problems of Creation,
for instance, as did his theological treatises. They implied
simply a more direct way of looking at the question, since
there they stood before us, so greatly and clearly a part of
His artistry. They were refreshing too because they provided material for a different branch of study, and as he
said once, he believed in a change of subject as the best
relaxation of the mind. Naturally too they took the place
to some extent of friends. Human friends 'were something
of a mixed blessing' to a man devoted to his work. Almost
he could say that he had not the time for them, as he had
time for mountains, which did not make the same demands.
Certainly his studies prospered. Doctor with distinction of
Philosophy, Theology and Canon Law, he found a quick
succession of posts readily offered, until he settled in 1884
as assistant to Dr Ceriani at the Ambrosian Library. As
librarian he did the climbs described in articles which now
go to make his book.

The reader is struck first with the scientific tone of
Achille Ratti's account of his traverse of Monte Rosa in
1889. It may be true, as Douglas Freshfield wrote, that
'Mgr. Ratti's patriotism made him eager that this spectacu-
lar feat should be repeated by his countrymen'. But only a
biographer very unversed in mountaineering lore could
have written of 'his real impatience at caution'. In reality,
in order to ascend this east face of Monte Rosa safely and
to make the first crossing to Zermatt by an Italian party,
he and his guide Gadin studied with great thoroughness
both previous accounts and the weather and snow conditions necessary for success. It was to be done 'not indeed
without difficulty, which is impossible, but without
danger'. 'The idea of attempting a gambler's throw never
once entered our heads.' His whole account is in some sense
a generous defence of the greatly abused Italian face, and

an assurance that it can be climbed safely. The party took much longer than they expected, because they insisted on a safer, more tedious route. But they were never in danger. They were benighted near the summit of the Dufourspitze, at a height of over 15,000 feet. He does not complain, though it was a cold night. Indeed the reverse, for 'who would have slept in that pure air? . . . We felt ourselves to be in the presence of a novel and most inspiring revelation of the omnipotence and majesty of God. How could we even think of the fatigue we had endured, much less complain of it?' Next morning they descended from the summit to search for Professor Grasselli's axe, which had been lost. Upon the spur of the moment they decided to cross the Zumsteinjoch, the col between the Dufourspitze and the next summit, the Zumsteinspitze. They made the first crossing of this pass, almost the highest in the Alps, on the day after their long climb, to spend another night out very near the comfortable beds of the Riffel. Here they even 'slept peacefully'.

The capacity to sit out quietly in discomfort was an asset of other mountaineering pastors, of men like the Rev. Hudson and his English peers who were among the most energetic pioneers of last century. They accepted such misadventures, when they befell, and enjoyed them. 'Even if our present predicament could be called unfortunate,' Achille Ratti wrote once, 'it was only right and reasonable to put a good face upon it.' If you believe mountains to be the direct work of the Omnipotent Creator, you will welcome 'the indescribable beauty of the surroundings, and the assured possibility of priceless experiences, which can only be enjoyed during a somewhat lengthy sojourn on the highest peaks, and then only at hours when one is least wont to be there'. These hours, it must be acknowledged, are not the most comfortable. Nor will you fret at delay and benightment, for you will recognize how small and unimportant are your movements in the great scheme of things of which you are witness. Thus, when Ratti's party was caught a few days later and compelled to spend a night below the shoulder of the Matterhorn, he could write: 'We resigned ourselves to passing the night where we were, not only without regret, but, I venture to say, with considerable enjoyment.' He remarks that it was a night 'in some ways even more wonderful than the one I spent a week before, quite near the top of Monte Rosa'. For what could inspire greater wonder than a view, at night, of the huge monuments which the Creator had erected? The whole structure fitted, was part of a manifest design.

The mountaineer who has seen San Pietro in Vaticano and Bernini's Colonnade, both of them so huge, yet so graceful and harmonious, so diverse in their separate parts, yet so easy in their grand simplicity to assemble under the eye in one comprehensive view,—that mountaineer knows that here too it is ever in the imitation of Nature that our art shows closest kinship with that of God, the first creator of all beautiful things.

Ratti, it has been said, might have become a fine scientist. He brought a love of accuracy and his inquiring spirit into the mountains. It is in repose upon the tops, or when benightment forces inactivity, that he has leisure to apply his science to worship. The expedition over Monte Rosa was undertaken in a spirit of scientific study; he pauses at many points to discuss questions of height, weather and the routes taken by previous parties. Some of his observations are made in the hope of defending the expedition and the construction of the Marinelli hut from charges of danger-seeking. But his interest strikes very much more deeply. And it is the same when he describes the descent of Mont Blanc by the Dôme Glacier, or the 'Misadventure in Spring' which befell Gadin and the Prince Gonzaga. In this chapter he gives details of the forms of treatment for frostbite. We look for the reason for his interest, and we find the scientific way viewed as our human approach to the Creator's works. Throughout the rest of his life, even

Monte Rosa

when he was debarred from active climbing, he continued an enthusiasm which was satisfying because founded, not on a sudden passion, but on scientific investigation of loved and revered objects. His feeling for mountains did not fade when the opportunity for visiting them ceased.

It was now however necessary to return to the Ambrosian Library. The years between 1884 and 1910, when he left Milan to assist the Prefect of the Vatican Library, increased his scholarship but blocked the outlets for physical activity. The facts of his career are well known. He proved an expert and scholarly librarian, and was responsible for the reorganization and cataloguing which gained him the knighthood of the Order of Saints Maurice and Lazarus. He published a number of works himself, chiefly about the library. At the same time he continued parish work, educating the urchins of San Sepolcro near the Ambrosian. In 1907 he was appointed Head of the Library in succession to Dr Ceriani. He was almost immediately transferred to Rome, to assist the Prefect of the Vatican Library, and he remained there through the war years until he was sent in 1918, to the surprise of all, as Apostolic Visitor to Warsaw. He showed energy in taking care of the affairs of Polish Catholics and courage in the face of the Bolshevist invasion. In 1921 he was recalled to Rome, and in the same year received the Cardinal's hat and the Archbishopric of Milan. In 1922 Pope Benedict XV died. Ratti was elected Pope, to all the world's surprise, on the first vote. His first act was to unfurl the Papal standard which had lain unused since 1870, the year when the Pope became a virtual prisoner in the Vatican. He thus announced the return of the Papacy to political power, and to a relationship with the Quirinal which culminated in the Lateran Agreement of 1929 with Mussolini. The negotiating of the agreement was a feat of which the Pope himself said: 'So great have been the difficulties in bringing this treaty to a successful conclusion, that I am tempted to think that a solution could only be achieved by a Pope who was also an Alpinist accustomed to tackling most arduous ascents.'

The eye of fancy wanders over this career of scholar-priest, hoping to spy a link between his early mountain activity and later elevation in the spiritual hierarchy. Achille Ratti's last ascent of a physical mountain was that of Vesuvius in 1899. It would be tempting to believe that the enthusiasm which fired the 1889 climbs lived into the next century, in whatever form. Clearly it lived still in his reading, for he 'never allowed an article on mountaineering or any record of an Alpine climb to pass unread and un-studied'. Thus the Alps in one obvious sense were an escape, since their literature eased the burden of more scholarly tasks. Besides this, the recollection of their beauty may have helped to block one gap left in the life of a celibate priest. And the restlessness which drives men over them may have prompted his surprising entry at an advanced age from the library into public life. It had seemed strange enough to some that he should choose to spend his leisure teaching the Catechism to illiterate boys. But he did more, he travelled to England. He agreed sud-denly, though against his will, to become Apostolic Visitor to Warsaw. This was an adventure and an activity whose difficulties he could face with a straight courage. He was recalled and became Archbishop of Milan. Even before his Papacy he had insisted on the 'international and super-national sovereignty of the Pope'. It would be going too far to trace in the first blows that he struck for the return of Papal power, from the raising of the Papal standards on-ward, a resolution bred of Alpine experience. Yet it is possible that dreaming of those heights, sublimating them in some sense into silent witnesses of his work, he deter-mined upon an act that should be worthy of their approval. It is easy to criticize his later reconciliation with Mussolini in the Lateran Agreement, which gave the Papacy a status on condition of its recognition of the Fascist régime. But he was not the only one to be deluded by Italy's apparent prosperity under a dictator; besides, the Pope's unique position demanded extreme caution. All that concerns us is that he himself had no doubts about the wisdom of his action, he worked with all his might to secure the Agreement and he considered it, as we have seen, worthy of a Pope who had accustomed himself to physical as well as diplomatic acrobatics.

The late Pope then was one example of the scholar-mountaineer. But he was also a Catholic priest. With him the mountains were an escape, not away from but into reality, since they were a part of God's most intimate handiwork. He could crowd into the magical corner of his mind occupied by them the longings, frustrations, dreams of beauty, which the average priestly librarian might placidly have smothered over or ignored. At the same time he drew from their treasure store restless energy which drove him out of the library, to parish work, to travel, to the Papacy. It was not surprising that the Papal attendants later puffed their remonstrance at the speed with which he covered the Vatican gardens. They were accustomed to a more comfortable pace in their Popes. He drew besides a stimulus to worship; the hills continued to give indisputable evidence of the power of their Creator. He drew the spirit of adventure which beset him when he had retired so far into his library that he thought himself unassailable. Pope Benedict XV, unmoved at his excuses and evasions when it was suggested that he should go as Apostolic Visitor to Warsaw, got up. He said: 'When can you start?'

'Tomorrow morning.'

Robert Falcon Scott: the Antarctic Tragedy

The ways of Providence are inscrutable, but there must be some reason why such a young, vigorous and promising life should be taken.

THE stuff of great narrative is woven rather of tragic failure than successful accomplishment. Thucydides' history could not move us so had the Athenians conquered in Sicily. To make literature of narrative writing there is needed a sublimation of the factual story until it enters that realm of the Universal which can be called 'great'. Scott is a writer whose own life was by the world's reckoning a failure, since he did not live to complete his expedition and was responsible directly for the loss of five lives. He must be contrasted with the successful Amundsen, who reached the Pole first just because his object was above all things efficiently to reach the Pole. Yet through the brave façade of his diary viewed against the background of impending failure, Scott will shine great where Amundsen is ephemeral. There is a new light shed upon him. It does not matter that we want at every step to clear him of the charge of faulty organization. 'The desire to excuse Scott

[149]

will be universal.' Thus does J. Gordon Hayes, in *Antarctica*, preface his criticisms. For we must come to see that it is the force of the diaries themselves that creates this universal desire. Indeed most English readers are brought up with a start, in Evans's critical comments after the last journey, with his apology: 'It seems a very cruel thing to say this, but there's no good in shutting one's eyes to the Truth, however unpleasantly clad she may be.' No, let Scott stand as a maker of mistakes; let his deeds shine poetically bright as the glorious, imbecile exploit of the Light Brigade. Then let him be great as a writer. At the same time let it be asked whether there was enough of mountain feeling in him to warrant his place in a gathering of mountain personalities; whether the fire burned bright of itself, or whether he faced hills and glaciers as no more than the obstacles to his endeavour.

There is no need to go back over his boyhood. It is known so well now that he was pigeon-chested and frail, and that his parents were concerned about his health. Let us take him past the year, 1887, when Sir Clements Markham picked him out as a promising young midshipman; past 1899 when he applied, almost by chance, to command the proposed Antarctic expedition and was almost by chance, as it seemed, appointed. The *Discovery* set sail on 31st of July 1901, and returned to England on 10th of September 1903. Between these dates much had happened. Winter quarters were established on Ross Island, under Mount Erebus. Erebus itself has had a special significance in Antarctic exploration, ever since Sir James Ross first caught sight of it, a volcano of fire and smoke in all that land of ice and snow. It seemed fitting that it should preside over the installation of a great British expedition on the island; for it is a land that was to have a peculiarly British association during the next twelve years.

Thus was the stage set for the spring and summer

journeys, and the scenery, as the sun slowly returned, answered proudly. From Crater Hill

the eye has passed on to scan that great frowning range of mountains to the west which has looked down on us in such ghostly, weird fashion throughout the winter months. Seen now in daylight, what a wild confusion of peaks and precipices, foothills, snowfields and glaciers it presents. . . . But northward of the west these lofty ridges fall again, and the ranges which stretch on beyond till they are lost in the fiery glow of the sun are lower than the monstrous pile to the west. Perhaps it is in this direction that we shall conquer the western land.

And so it was.

The first long journey, however, was to the south, in the company of Shackleton and Dr Wilson. The peaks towards the Beardmore Glacier were examined, and the future route to the Pole. But it was left to Shackleton, eight years later, to complete the discovery of the route by a difficult climb up Mount Hope. From the ridge 'there burst upon our view an open road to the south, for there stretched before us a great glacier, the Beardmore, running almost south and north, between two huge mountain ranges'. Scott's way then was ready for him. It was only after another winter spent at Hut Point that Scott passed to the western land. But the Southern Journey itself was filled with a vision of mountains, and with a mode of life that belongs to the mountaineer as well as to the Polar explorer. At the end of the first volume of *The Voyage of the 'Discovery'* he has described with a strange realism the vividness of sledging miseries; the long and weary march, the cold night when it is a painful effort to turn over, still more painful to look at the watch and see whether it is time to get up: the hours spent inactive in a blizzard, with no escape: 'Now and again conversation breaks out; someone tells a droll tale of his infancy; the tale carries us away to other times for a space, forgetful of our miserable surroundings; but the effort flickers and dies, and gradually thought creeps back to the present.' Even so have mountaineers lain inactive and uneasy in their sleeping-bags.

Polar life is not tinged now with so gruelling a hardship. As it is described, for instance, by Colin Bertram, camping can be positively a comfortable business. Many of Scott's 'miseries' are no more. The three suffered too from pangs of hunger as they made their way south, mapping the mountainous boundary of the Ross Barrier. These were due to a faulty and insufficient diet. But so convincing is Scott's account that we do not see that a proportion of this torture was of his own making, and this in part because of the critical question of dogs. It is not true that he altogether neglected the possibilities of dogs, though it is certain that he developed 'an unconquerable aversion' to their use. He did not like to treat them, as Nansen and Peary and later Amundsen treated them, the 'inhumane' way, but he most certainly did use them. On the first days out they travelled so fast that the men sat back on the sledges. Unhappily the fish on which they were fed was rotten, the dogs failed and died, and Scott acquired that aversion to their use which later cost his life. Gordon Hayes has maintained:

All this is simply pathetic now, for dogs do not suffer when they are properly treated. They were made to be man's servants, while man was not created as a beast of burden. Scott never saw this until it was too late; for he had no experience of modern dog transport until his last expedition, and his gentle heart would not bear to inflict the suffering that he had imagined previously to be inevitable in the use of dogs.

This is a trifle unfair to Scott, but certainly through their failure was inflicted upon himself and his companions the pain and hunger which he greatly describes. We see with our own eyes Shackleton's drawn face as he staggered back from the Southern Journey, or Wilson sketching snowblind before his tent.

There were of course compensations, as the magnificent mountain range unfolded itself to their right. 'One of the most glorious mountain scenes we have yet witnessed.' 'Pelion heaped on Ossa.' 'We have decided that we have

Mount Erebus as Wind Vane

found something fitting to bear the name of him whom we must always the most delight to honour, and "Mount Markham" it shall be called, in memory of the father of the expedition.' For Scott looked often at his mountains with the eye of romance. They stood as symbolic landmarks and signposts to his journeys, heavenly sponsors of human endeavour. They are always finely pictured. The party then tried to reach the land, cutting steps across an ice chasm, but this proved impossible. Their return was a heroic struggle, largely because of the shortage of food. They could think and talk of nothing else in their hunger, and in Shackleton's sickness lies drama; it was a splendid feat to get him back alive. Once again the narrative is so impressive that the enchanted reader forgets Stefansson's verdict that 'adventures on a modern expedition are generally a sign of incompetence'. Let us have the incompetence, if we are allowed the tale of such adventure.

After a second winter at Hut Point on Ross Island the most important journey, with Lashly and Edgar Evans and man-hauled sledges, was up the Ferrar Glacier. This led through the mountains to the west and over the ice plateau which is the inland part of South Victoria Land. The entrance to the glacier was impressive: 'Towering precipitously between three and four thousand feet above our heads are the high, sunlit pinnacles of the Cathedral Rocks . . . their lofty peaks might well be the spires of some mighty edifice.' There is never a desire expressed, be it noted, to climb these peaks. But who could contemplate such a wish, under the conditions which he endured? It was a hard enough job getting safely through the crevasses of the glacier; Desolation Camp, at which they spent a storm-bound week, was a 'nightmare'. They reached the plateau and continued a further 200 miles before they turned. It had been a magnificent achievement, and the finest single piece of man-hauled sledging at that time accomplished, with the ever-present possibility of a new sea appearing dramatically the other side of the Cap. But they were glad to turn, in the immense wilderness. 'It has been so for countless years, and will be so for countless more. And we, little human insects, have started to crawl over this awful desert, and are now bent on crawling back again. Could anything be more terrible than this silent, wind-swept immensity when one thinks such thoughts?' For once Scott relates the human being directly to the larger scene which he is observing.

The adventures of the return were again misadventures, this time of mountaineering. First Lashly slipped, and the whole party with their sledge slid some 300 feet on to the glacier up which they had earlier climbed. A short while after this Scott and Evans fell through into a crevasse, and found themselves 'dangling at the end of the trace, with blue walls on either side and a very horrid-looking gulf below'. 'There was nothing for it but to climb the rope. It is some time since I swarmed a rope, and to have to do so in thick clothes and heavy crampons, and with frost-bitten fingers seemed to me in the nature of the impossible.' But it was done, and the party assembled in safety on the glacier. The crevasse might conceivably have been avoided had still greater care been taken. That is not ours to decide. The narration of the effort to escape holds us entranced. Scott continued, undaunted, to explore Dry Valley and to return safely to the ship. Erebus greeted them from afar, as it has greeted many a party. Evans's 'White Lady of the South, with a film of gauze wrapped around her wonderful shoulders' was a symbol of hope and comfort. It was always a sign of home when the summit came into view, even if it were 90 or 100 miles off. A party from Shackleton's expedition later climbed, under difficult conditions, this mountain which he describes as standing 'sentinel at the gate of the Great Ice Barrier . . . a magnificent picture'. And on Scott's last expedition, when Crean and Lashly were pulling back the apparently dying Evans, they raised him on the sledge to catch a first glimpse of the 13,000-foot summit. It was a sign of hope that he could see it—and Scott himself never saw it in 1912 as he did when he returned now in 1902.

Let us then leave him at the close of this expedition peacefully watching penguins near Cape Royds: 'Words fail me to describe what a delightful spot this is. . . . Erebus towers high above us on our right, and to the left we look away over the long stretch of fast ice to the cloud-capped western mountains.'

It is Scott the writer who is to be judged, not the bearer from his journey of precious scientific results. Of his book Gordon Hayes has written: 'There is a fascination that is missing in Scott's last Journal. His earlier book leaves nothing to be desired. It is lucid, happy and bright, with the delightfulness of youth.' Certainly there is an assurance of success in it, yet an assurance which has allowed at times a stylishness, almost an affectation. The stock, conventional phrases come creeping in. The wind 'is straining our threadbare tent in no reassuring manner'. Or 'it must not be imagined that our route was all plain sailing and easy travelling'. There is no time for such word-building in the last Journal. *The Voyage of the 'Discovery'* is delightful. The Journal of the 1910–12 expedition is great, and not least because of its terseness and the sense hanging over it that the writer will not live to amplify his tale. 'The Journal contains so much sorrow and complaint, as if the shadow of the end was being cast backward along the writer's path almost from the beginning of the last expedition.' That is true, and we are prepared to make all the reservations that Mr Gordon Hayes requires when we pry into Scott's thoughts. 'We should remember that the publication of any sensitive man's private diary is an extremely severe temperamental test. And it must be read, not only sympathetically, but with a certain reverence for the pulsations of the human heart.' Certainly, but it is

[155]

these very pulsations which go to make Tragedy; no 'want of unity' can destroy this astounding quality in the work.

The want of unity is inevitable. This time the objects of the expedition are not explicitly stated; the book has come to us badly edited. In scientific results he achieved much. 'The greatest and most enduring merit of this expedition consisted, not in the attainment of the Pole, but in the attention devoted to the advancement of science' (J. Gordon Hayes). Had Scott confined himself to scientific exploration all might have been well. But he intended also to march for the Pole, without Amundsen's advantages. He wrote himself: 'If he gets to the Pole it must be before we do, as he is bound to travel fast with dogs.' The question springs to mind, 'Why have you not got them?' Why not, instead of the motley collection of transport which Apsley Cherry Garrard christened 'the Baltic fleet'? Yet in spite or because of this and every other instance of 'extremely bad organization' (Cherry Garrard) Scott's diary will be read over and again. With Amundsen's account, exciting as it is, the reader is concerned but once.

The hand of fate is accused very early in the story, during a calm met with on the way to Ross Island. 'I begin to wonder if fortune will ever turn her wheel. On every possible occasion she seems to have decided against us.' But the party arrived safely at its winter quarters, again under Mount Erebus, 'so that always towering above us we have the grand snowy peak with its snowy summit'. Before winter set in depots were laid on the southern route for next summer. Of that journey Scott wrote his 'Impressions':

The small green tent and the great white road.
The driving clouds of powdered snow.
The crunch of footsteps which break the surface crust.
The windblown furrows.
The blue arch beneath the smoky cloud.
The drift snow like finest flour penetrating every hole and corner.

The blizzard, Nature's protest, the crevasse, Nature's pitfall . . . the light rippled snow bridge gives no warning of the hidden danger, its position unguessable until man or beast is floundering, clawing and struggling for foothold on the brink. . . .

Such poetic impressions he had leisure to assimilate and record during the quiet winter. The party entertained itself with lectures, and after them Scott reflected upon such themes as the new interest in exploration which his own expedition proclaimed, and not only in the exploration of the Poles:

The expansion of human interest in rude surroundings may perhaps best be illustrated by comparisons. It will serve to recall such a simple case as the fact that our ancestors applied the terms horrid, frightful, to mountain crags which in our own day are more justly admired as lofty, grand and beautiful. The poetic conception of this natural phenomenon has followed not so much an inherent change of sentiment as the intimacy of wider knowledge and the death of superstitious influence.

But the night of winter passed, the time was come for action and the brief message, for the long-prepared attempt upon the Pole itself. One word therefore must be said about the organization of this last journey, that we may ponder whether Scott was right that 'our luck in the weather [for instance] is preposterous'. Then we shall appreciate, whether or not this was so, the literary quality of the last diary that records such luck.

The mistake over dogs has been sufficiently noted. He never fully understood that they could be used without inhumanity and over difficult country, as Amundsen showed. Indeed they were most suitable for glacier work, since they are lighter than men and the weight is more evenly distributed. There was certainly a mistaken feeling of pity; partly, too, Scott may have felt subconsciously that it would be a finer thing to reach the Pole by unaided human effort. He would have preferred to climb his Everest without oxygen. Thus he started on the Polar journey from Cape Evans with four forms of transport, and reduced these gradually to one. His sentiments about animals and his indecision, even if we admire them, killed him; if he had trusted to dogs alone he would never have had to postpone his start by a month for the ponies' sake. And he seemed almost to know it. He wrote in a letter to his wife before starting: 'It seems a woeful long time since I saw your face, and there is the likelihood of a woefuller time ahead, and then what?' He complained, we have seen, of the weather, and contrasted his fortune, on the glacier, with Shackleton's before him. Yet statistical tables show that he enjoyed better weather than either Shackleton or Amundsen. Again, the snow: 'The soft snow in the lower reaches of the glacier [the Beardmore] again reduced pace.' He forgot that the heavy fall had covered the crevasses, so that he experienced almost no difficulty with them. 'We have not seen such alarming crevasses as I had expected.' It is as though he was determined that luck must be against him, while yet his skill and his will to live increased with the difficulties. Apsley Cherry Garrard describes him at work on the glacier:

There is no doubt that Scott knows where to aim for in a glacier, as it was just here that Shackleton had two or three of his worst days' work in such a maze of crevasses. . . . Scott avoids the sides of a glacier and goes nowhere near the snow; he often heads straight for apparent chaos, and somehow when we appear to have reached a cul-de-sac we find an open road.

The expedition, then, continued up the glacier. Scott comments in a matter-of-fact way of the crevasses that 'we all had falls into them, Atkinson and Teddy Evans going down the length of their harness'. At the same time he combines in a rare manner annoyance at the glacier's irregularities with a quite dispassionate interest in their cause.

On top of this we got on the most extraordinary surface,—narrow crevasses ran in all directions. They were quite invisible, being covered with a thin crust of hardened névé without a sign of a crack in it. We all fell in one after the other and sometimes two together. We have had many unexpected falls before, but usually through being unable to mark the run of the surface appearance of the cracks or where such cracks are covered with soft snow. How a hardened crust can form a crack is a real puzzle,—it seems to argue extremely slow movement.

Or when one of the party falls deeply he notes that 'it was
fifty feet deep and eight feet across, in form U, showing
that the word "unfathomable" can rarely be applied'. But
finally they were on the Polar plateau itself, some 10,000
feet up, and the last of the long plods had begun. On
4th of January 1912 the last supporting party returned.
Scott and four companions were left with man-hauled
sledges. On January 16th they saw a flag left by the Norwegians and knew that they had been forestalled. They
had never openly 'raced', yet they felt now all the vexation
of Carrel upon the Matterhorn. 'It is a terrible disappoint-
ment and I am very sorry for my loyal companions. Many
thoughts come and much discussion have we had.' The
Pole, the summit of long hope, seemed now far from the
friendly spot which Amundsen cheerfully describes. 'Great
God! This is an awful place and terrible enough for us to
have laboured to it without the reward of priority.' That
day's entry ends: 'Now for the run home and a desperate
struggle. I wonder if we can do it.' Amundsen had had no
such doubts. For the foreboding of the last months,
accumulated, seemed to break now in this wave of disappointed pride. It is as if Scott was already beaten when he
turned from the goal, back to '800 miles of solid dragging
—and goodbye to most of the day-dreams'.

The details of the return journey are shadowed with a
sense of tragic doom. The high altitude at a very low
temperature must have begun to worry them, though it is
never mentioned, for they had been pulling for a long
period at about 10,000 feet. Now they reach the Beardmore Glacier again and once, when they step out on to a
cheerful rock under Mount Buckley, the tension is relaxed.
Wilson sits in the sun and sketches. But very soon after
they are lost in a maze of crevasses, and the description of
their frustrating perversity is among Scott's most dramatic
writing.

There were times when it seemed almost impossible to find a way out of the awful turmoil in which we found ourselves. At length, arguing that there must be a way on our left, we plunged in that direction. It got worse, however, more icy and crevassed. We could not manage our ski and pulled on foot, falling into crevasses every minute, —most luckily no bad accident.

They were driven on now by the desperate need to reach the next food depot, and yet they were weakening all the time, even when they had the food. Evans died the first, partly from his fall into a crevasse. Yet such is the force and authority of the Journal that this death sounds to the reader like a sudden, shocking trumpet call. Things had seemed difficult—but by no means desperate. The conditions were bad—but not hopeless. Snow had become like 'desert sand'—but only now do we pull up with a start, and realize that it may be Scott's own tiredness which creates such difficulties. We look back over the statistics to compare the conditions with Amundsen's, and find to our surprise that Amundsen's were worse. For by now Scott's party was weakening daily, and the end hovers indeed. 'God help us, we can't keep up this pulling, that is certain. Amongst ourselves we are unendingly cheerful, but what each man feels in his heart I can only guess.' Hayes sums up: 'The pulling, it was there that tragedy lay. For over three months, day after day, and with no Sunday's rest, Scott and his companions tugged at their sledges. They literally hauled like horses, till they dropped in their tracks.'

The comparison of Scott's book with Amundsen's is instructive. Mr Stephen Gwynn has written that

in that tragedy Scott and not Amundsen dominates. The victor slips away, having vanquished not only the Antarctic but his rival in the attempt; it is left to Scott to make mankind feel and understand and see what the approach to that goal meant. Nothing that Amundsen has written or could have written makes us aware of his achievement as do the pages of Scott's Journal.

There is a certain uncritical admiration in this reflection, but it strikes near the truth. Amundsen's account is very readable; but it is read with that enjoyment which we owe to many a successful adventure. It is not remembered. His expedition was a masterpiece of organization. 'This enterprise was one of the most perfect exhibitions of man's supremacy over Nature.' For Amundsen had made the attainment of the Pole itself his object. His route was shorter but more difficult than Scott's, and he had organized every unit to the one end of overcoming those difficulties. Relying on dogs the Norwegians travelled very quickly up and down the hazardous Devil's Glacier, sometimes forced to reconnoitre with a rope, sometimes marching through blizzards because delay irked them. Of the Pole itself Amundsen writes: 'After this we proceeded to the greatest and most solemn act of the whole journey—the planting of our flag.' For as Nansen said, this was 'a victory of human mind and human strength over the dominion and powers of Nature'. It was a victory for Norway; it did not include, as did Scott's expedition, a painstaking and sympathetic inquiry into her secrets. Amundsen's scientific results were slight enough—though with his huge supplies of food he could have afforded a larger staff. Again and again is the reader of his story struck with the limited nature of his objective; he seems to 'drive furiously' through the Antarctic, pausing only from time to time to wonder at the strange beauty that is around him.

Scott is great because he elevated his own journey in scope from the particular to the Universal. Human life is at its best a blundering attempt to harness Nature to our chariot, to succeed in high attempts or to go down courageously. It is a companionship in which sacrifice is made, life even is laid down, for friends. It is a brave front to the inevitable. These qualities Scott showed superlatively, and nowhere so touchingly as in the last 'Message to the Public' and the last letters, written while he was slowly dying. If there is little that can be technically called 'religious' in them, there is that necessary and great quality of all religion, loving thought for the community

L   [161]

and the desire to express reverence before a Power which is, ultimately, merciful. 'The great God has called me . . . not perhaps believing in all that you hold to so splendidly, but still believing that there is a God—a merciful God.' Or of the dying Wilson he writes: 'His eyes have a comfortable blue look of hope, and his mind is peaceful with the satisfaction of his faith in regarding himself as part of the great scheme of the Almighty.' He believes in such a scheme, but it is not for him to answer what is his own part. It is enough that in simply putting the question, in those circumstances in which he died, he ennobled it. Whatever may be known and thought of his expedition, of his scientific results and his organization, the story of the last journey has a deeper meaning. It is for this reason that Gwynn can claim: 'His supreme achievement is that he touched the imagination of his country as no other man has done during the course of this century.' This too is why letters from the trenches poured in to his widow, from men who had no experience of exploration but had been moved to courage by his narrative. This is why it is not inappropriate that he should be included here among our literary mountaineers. His life's end was strangely shadowed by mountains, mountains that have appeared already as the background to much of his travel. His own character, we have seen, was touched and inspired by their presence. And moreover the quality of his writing suggests a direction for the mountain chronicles of the future. They will continue to be the relation of fine action, simple and yet with a sense of its ultimate significance in human life. Huge tracts of the world's surface remain to be explored, in Central Asia and at the Pole. Their exploration needs no 'literary' men, only that quality of greatness which it has enjoyed in the past. If the explorers have the humanity of Scott, they too can be the writers of a story that moves the heart because it elevates their journeys until they become a message to all men.

A SHORT BIBLIOGRAPHY

DANTE AND PETRARCH (see note to Chapter II).
  Dante's *Divine Comedy* and *Canzoni*.
  Curiosità Dantesche, by P. Bellezza.
  Petrarch: *Epist. Famil.*, L, iv, ep. 1.
  Le Rime.
  Il Petrarca Alpinista, by G. Carducci.
  Studi sul Petrarca, by P. Zumbini.
  Rivista del Club Alpino Italiano, 1937, bibliography by P. Guiton.
  Alpine Journal, vol. x, D. W. Freshfield on 'Dante'.
  Petrarca Letterato, by G. Billanovich.

JEAN-JACQUES ROUSSEAU.
  Les Confessions.
  Les Rêveries d'un Promeneur Solitaire.
  Comments *passim* in Sainte-Beuve.
  Jean-Jacques Rousseau, the Child of Nature, by J. Charpentier.

H. B. DE SAUSSURE.
  Voyages dans les Alpes.
  Horace Bénédict de Saussure, by D. W. Freshfield.
  Many articles in journals scientific and Alpine.

GOETHE.
  Poems. Letters.
  Dichtung und Wahrheit.
  Goethe, by Georg Brandes.
  Goethe, by Emil Ludwig.
  Petrarca e Goethe Alpinisti, by P. Lioy.
  Notes to Goethe's Poems, by J. D. Boyd.

THE WORDSWORTHS.
  The Poems of William Wordsworth, especially the '*Prelude*' (ed. E.
      de Selincourt).
  The Journals of Dorothy Wordsworth.
  A Guide through the District of the Lakes—W. Wordsworth.
  Wordsworth's View of Nature and its Ethical Consequences, by N.
      Lacey.
  Wordsworth's Youth, by Leslie Stephen.
  Dorothy Wordsworth, a Biography, by E. de Selincourt.
  The Picturesque, by Christopher Hussey.

A Short Bibliography

JOHN KEATS AND THE ROMANTICS.
The Poems and Letters of John Keats.
Shelley *passim*—in particular 'Mont Blanc'.
Byron *passim*—in particular *Childe Harold*.
John Keats, by J. Middleton Murry.
The Decline and Fall of the Romantic Ideal, by F. L. Lucas.

JOHN RUSKIN.
Sesame and Lilies.
Modern Painters, vol. iv.
Praeterita.
Letters to Effie Gray.
John Ruskin, by E. T. Cook.

LESLIE STEPHEN.
Studies of a Biographer ('In Praise of Walking').
The Playground of Europe.
Leslie Stephen—biography by W. H. Maitland.
Leslie Stephen, by N. Annan.

FRIEDRICH NIETZSCHE.
Thus Spake Zarathustra.
Beyond Good and Evil.
The Letters of Friedrich Nietzsche.
'Der Bergsteiger Friedrich Nietzsche' by Herr Sepp Walcher
    (articles in *Swiss Alpine Journal*, 1948).
The Problem of Theism, by A. C. Pigou.
Friedrich Nietzsche, Philosopher of Culture, by F. Coplestone.

POPE PIUS XI.
Scritti Alpinistici (translated by J. E. C. Eaton as *Climbs on Alpine
    Peaks*).
Pope Pius XI, a Biography, by W. and L. Townsend.

ROBERT FALCON SCOTT.
The Voyage of the 'Discovery'.
Scott's Last Expedition.
The Worst Journey in the World, by A. Cherry Garrard.
With Scott: the Silver Lining, by Griffith Taylor.
South with Scott, by E. R. G. R. Evans.
The Great White South, by H. G. Ponting.
Antarctic Adventure, by R. E. Priestley.
Antarctica, by J. Gordon Hayes.
The Conquest of the South Pole, by J. Gordon Hayes.
Captain Scott, by S. Gwynn.

This book is set in 12 on 13-point Bell, a type face designed by the printer, publisher, and letter-founder John Bell and originally cut for his British Letter Foundry in 1788 by Richard Austin.

A specimen of the original type which has been rediscovered by Mr Stanley Morrison in the Bibliothèque Nationale is described by him as the first English modern face. It has the characteristics of the class of moderns, the flat serifs and vertical stress; and yet it lacks the rigidity of other moderns of its period which followed mathematical rather than artistic principles.

The recut of this type face, based on the punches discovered in the twenties in Messrs Stephenson & Blake's foundry, was undertaken in 1931 by the Monotype Corporation from whose matrices this book has been cast.